OZARKS GUNFIGHTS & OTHER NOTORIOUS INCIDENTS

OZARKS GUNFIGHTS AND OTHER NOTORIOUS INCIDENTS

Larry Wood

PELICAN PUBLISHING COMPANY
GRETNA 2010

The word "Pelican" and the depiction of a pelican
are trademarks of Pelican Publishing Company, Inc.,
and are registered in the U.S. Patent and Trademark Office.

Library of Congress Cataloging-in-Publication Data

Wood, Larry (Larry E.)
Ozarks gunfights and other notorious incidents / Larry Wood.
p. cm.
Includes bibliographical references and index.
ISBN 978-1-58980-703-7 (pbk. : alk. paper) 1. Ozark
Mountains—History—Anecdotes. 2. Outlaws—Ozark
Mountains—Biography—Anecdotes. 3. Criminals—Ozark
Mountains—Biography—Anecdotes. 4. Crime—Ozark
Mountains—History—Anecdotes. 5. Violence—Ozark
Mountains—History—Anecdotes. 6. Ozark Mountains—
Biography—Anecdotes. 7. Ozark Mountains—History, Local—
Anecdotes. I. Title.
F417.O9W66 2009
976.7'1—dc22
2009039548

Printed in the United States of America
Published by Pelican Publishing Company, Inc.
1000 Burmaster Street, Gretna, Louisiana 70053

Contents

Preface

During the Civil War, loyalties were divided in the Ozarks, particularly in the slave-holding Union state of Missouri. Nowhere was the notion of brother fighting against brother or neighbor against neighbor, which is often associated with the Civil War, truer than it was in southwest Missouri and the Ozarks region. The divided loyalties gave rise to a vicious brand of guerrilla warfare that played itself out mostly as a series of raids and counterraids fueled by revenge and often characterized by atrocity.

Personal and political resentments lingered long after 1865, and lawlessness continued to plague the region throughout the latter half of the nineteenth century and into the twentieth, as bitter feelings left over from the war prompted or contributed to feuds and other violent clashes.

Casual observers often associate towns like Dodge City, Kansas, and Tombstone, Arizona, with the Wild West, but in the years immediately following the Civil War, the Ozarks were still very much a part of the West and nowhere was wilder than places like the mining town of Granby in southwest Missouri or the cow town of Baxter Springs, Kansas, on the region's western edge.

Then came the discovery of lead at various sites north and west of Granby, and booming mining towns like Joplin, Missouri, and Galena, Kansas, sprang up in the 1870s, drawing a parade of gamblers, prostitutes, and other ne'er-do-wells and ushering in a new wave of lawlessness. Joplin and some of the other towns of the mining district retained their wild, anything-goes reputations well into the twentieth century and became havens for lawbreakers during the gangster era of the 1920s and 1930s. Witness, for example, Bonnie and Clyde's shootout with police when their hideout in Joplin was discovered in the spring of 1933.

What follows are stories of some of the more notorious incidents that happened in the Ozarks between the end of the Civil War and approximately 1950 (a cutoff date I chose simply because anything more recent than that doesn't seem much like history to me).

Acknowledgments

Several of the chapters in this book (or versions thereof) were first published as articles in a variety of regional and national magazines or newspapers, and I'd like to acknowledge and thank those publications. They include the *Galena (KS) Sentinel, Kansas Heritage,* the *Ozarks Mountaineer,* the *Ozarks Reader, Springfield Magazine, True West Magazine,* and *Wild West Magazine.* I want to say a special thanks to Dr. Fred Pfister, editor of the *Ozarks Mountaineer,* and to Greg Lalire, editor of *Wild West Magazine,* both of whom worked with me on several of these articles.

This book has involved a lot of research, trips to various libraries and other archival facilities, interlibrary loans, and correspondence. In short, it has been a great deal of work, but it's the kind of work I love. Besides, I've had a lot of help along the way.

Let me first thank the staff at the Joplin Public Library, which has been the home base for most of my research and the library through which I have obtained materials on interlibrary loan. Other institutions or organizations that have played a part in the making of this book include the Barry County Museum, the Baxter Springs Heritage Center and Museum, the Carthage Public Library, the Cherokee County Genealogical-Historical Society Library, the Cherryvale Museum, the Christian County Library, the Galena Genealogical Library, the Granby Miners Museum, the Greene County Records Center and Archives, the Jasper County Records Center, the Kansas State Historical Society, the Missouri State Archives, the Missouri Southern State University Library, the Missouri State University Library, the Mt. Vernon Branch Library—Barry-Lawrence Regional Library, the Neosho/Newton County Library, Leonard H. Axe

Library—Pittsburg State University, the Springfield-Greene County Library, the State Historical Society of Missouri, and the University of Arkansas Library.

I can't begin to name all the individuals who have helped me in some way in my research for the book, but a few names come readily to mind: Nancy Brown, Linda Childers, Ramona Coleman, Patty Crane, John Durbin, Dixie Haase, Frankie Meyer, Marilyn Schmitt, Marilyn Smith, Steve Weldon, and Jason Sullivan. Thanks to all of you, and if I have left out anyone I should have mentioned, please know that it was inadvertent.

I also need to say a special word of thanks to William Preston Mangum II, who coauthored "The Younger Brothers' Roscoe Gun Battle" with me, for graciously allowing me to reprint the article as a chapter in this book.

In addition, I would like to thank Heather Green, assistant editor at Pelican, for her thorough and helpful edit. The book is better because of her able skill and advice.

Last but far from least, I thank my wife, G. G., for being both my best critic and my biggest supporter. She served as the first reader for most of the chapters in this book and offered invaluable advice, while at the same time offering steadfast encouragement. I love you, G. G.

OZARKS GUNFIGHTS AND OTHER NOTORIOUS INCIDENTS

1

Wild Bill Hickok's Springfield Shootout

In the late afternoon of July 21, 1865, James Butler Hickok, his .44 Colt dragoon at his side, waited near the corner of South Street on the public square in Springfield, Missouri, to confront Davis Tutt. Citizens of the town, aware of the bad blood between the two men, gaped eagerly from the shelter of buildings, like spectators at the Roman Coliseum anticipating a festival of violence. If Dave Tutt came across the square wearing the gold Waltham watch he had taken from Hickok earlier in the day, they knew there'd be hell to pay.

Near the beginning of the Civil War, J. B. Hickok had made a minor name for himself on the frontier for his part in the McCanles shootout in Nebraska Territory, and during the war, his adventures as a Union spy and scout enhanced his reputation. By the time he landed in southwest Missouri toward the end of the war, he had already earned the moniker "Wild Bill" and was known throughout the region as a man not to be trifled with. But it was not until a few months after the war, in the raucous town of Springfield, that the Hickok legend truly began.

During the latter part of the war, Hickok worked out of the Southwest District headquarters of the Union Department of the Missouri at Springfield, operating against bushwhackers and Southern partisans. During his wanderings throughout the region, he had made the acquaintance of Davis Tutt and struck up a friendship of sorts, despite the fact that Tutt was a former Confederate soldier. Sometime in the mid to later part of the war, Tutt and his family arrived in Springfield, and the two men became reacquainted.

In January of 1865, Tutt, known around town as a hard case, was sued for stealing a dark, iron-gray horse, but the Greene County Circuit Court merely ordered the defendant to return the animal to its rightful owner. About the same time, he got into trouble with the law over a charge of "gaming." Hickok's gambling activities had also drawn the attention of civil authorities, and like his card-playing buddy Tutt, Wild Bill had gained a reputation among some local citizens as a ruffian. In January, he and Tutt, along with two other men, signed a $1,000 bond together, bailing out a man named Larkin Russell after Russell was indicted for grand larceny.

Wild Bill Hickok (Courtesy Legends of America)

Shortly after this incident, though, Hickok left town on another scouting expedition. From Cassville on February 10, 1865, he wired the Southwest District commander, Brig. Gen. John B. Sanborn, at Springfield requesting directions as to his next movement. The following day, Sanborn sent him into Arkansas in the vicinity of Yellville, Tutt's old hometown, to spy on Confederate colonel Archibald S. Dobbin.

When Wild Bill returned to Springfield at the close of the war to take up residence, an unruly spirit fostered by the war still reigned in the area. During the war, loyalties in the border state of Missouri had been deeply divided, and the conflict had degenerated into a vicious brand of guerrilla warfare that gave rise to plunder, atrocity, and disorder. Springfield had been controlled by the Union throughout most of the war, but a significant minority of citizens in and around the town still held Southern sympathies. The recently negotiated peace had done little to assuage the old resentments.

Festering bitterness as well as the general atmosphere of chaos spawned by the war no doubt fueled some of the civilian complaints filed in May and June of 1865 with Union officials. Greene County citizens cited "lawless and disorderly conduct on the part of soldiers" and reported,

> Petty laundering and pilfering is carried on throughout the town and the adjoining country, and citizens are threatened and even fired at if they attempt to protect their property. Within the limits of this town . . . citizens are insulted and threatened by soldiers every night. Ladies are grossly insulted and the safety of every one endangered by the promiscuous firing so constantly indulged in.

In this atmosphere of mayhem, Tutt got himself arrested again, this time for "resisting civil officers." At his court appearance on July 20, he was fined $100 and ordered held "in custody of the sheriff until fine and costs are fully paid." The following day Tutt's attorney appeared before the court and had the verdict against his client set aside and a new trial granted. Tutt went straight back to the gambling table with

Wild Bill Hickok in an upstairs room of the Lyon House, a hotel just south of the square on South Street.

Friction between Hickok and Tutt, according to some reports, had been building for weeks. During the war, Wild Bill had met and courted a girl named Susannah Moore. They had recently broken up, and Dave Tutt had wasted no time wooing the young woman. Hickok exacted a measure of revenge by promptly turning his attention to Dave's sister, a courtship that displeased both Dave and his mother, who cared nothing for Yankees of any sort.

The growing hostility between the two men came to a head at the card table. Accounts differ as to exactly what happened. One report suggests that Tutt was not directly involved in the game that day, because hard feelings between the two men had already reached such a point that Hickok refused to play cards with Tutt. Tutt responded by trying to pick fights with Hickok and by bankrolling other gamblers so they could keep playing against Hickok. On the fateful day, Hickok won about $200 from one of Tutt's surrogates, infuriating Tutt.

Reports generally agree that when the game ended, Tutt demanded payment from Hickok of a previous debt, and the two men argued over the amount of the debt. Tutt said Wild Bill owed him $35, and Hickok claimed it was only $25. Refusing the lesser amount, Tutt then picked up Hickok's Waltham watch and vowed to hold it until the disputed debt was paid. Wild Bill warned Tutt not to wear the watch in public, but the nonchalant Tutt shrugged off the suggestion and said he aimed to wear it on the public square. "If you do," Hickok replied, "I'll shoot you, and I warn you not to come across the square with it on."

The two men parted company, and later that day Wild Bill showed up at the public square to carry out his threat if necessary. Bystanders told him that, yes, Tutt was somewhere downtown and, yes, he was wearing the watch. Thus began Hickok's determined vigil. Even as the more timid souls took cover, other men clustered around the gunfighter like greenhorn reporters. Would Tutt show? What would Bill do if he did show?

Soon Tutt's younger brother happened along, and Bill told him he'd better go tell Dave to take off the watch, but the young man replied that his brother had a right to wear whatever he pleased. Wild Bill repeated his grim warning, but before the brother could respond, Davis Tutt came out of the livery stable at the northwest corner of the square and started strolling toward the group. "There he comes now," Hickok announced.

The men around Bill scurried away as he stepped forward. When Tutt was in front of the courthouse, about seventy-five paces away, Hickok hollered, "Dave, don't you come across here with that watch."

The two men reached for their revolvers at about the same time and fired almost simultaneously, with Hickok using one arm as a prop for his weapon. Tutt, shot in the chest, staggered into the courthouse doorway, collapsed, and died almost immediately. The gun smoke had scarcely cleared when authorities showed up. Wild Bill handed over his

Springfield square today looking from where Hickok stood to where Tutt stood.

weapon and offered himself as a prisoner to military officers, who turned him over to the sheriff. A few minutes later, however, according to one critic, Hickok was "riding leisurely up South street." The *Missouri Weekly Patriot* of Springfield reported the shooting incident in its July 27 issue:

> David Tutt of Yellville, Arkansas was shot on the public square at 6 o'clock p.m. on Friday last by James B. Hickok, better known in Southwest Missouri as "Wild Bill." The difficulty occurred from a game of cards. Hickock [*sic*] is a native of Homer, Lasalle county, Illinois and is about twenty-six years of age. He has been engaged since his sixteenth year, with the exception of about two years, with Russell, Majors and Waddill [*sic*], in government service as scout, guide, or with exploring parties, and has rendered most efficient and signal service to the Union cause, as numerous acknowledgements from the different commanding officers with whom he has served will testify.

Indicted for manslaughter, Hickok came before the Greene County Circuit Court on Friday, August 4, with Col. R. W. Fyan serving as prosecutor, Congressman John S. Phelps (later Missouri governor) acting for the defense, and Judge Sempronius H. "Pony" Boyd presiding. The political atmosphere of the times colored the testimony of witnesses and imbued the entire court proceedings. The prosecutor tried to purge the proceedings of political overtones by asking the judge to instruct the jury to "disregard evidence as to the moral character of deceased, and as to his character for loyalty," but sides were quickly taken. Tutt's friends said Hickok lay in ambush for over an hour waiting to provoke a shootout. They claimed that he approached with his gun already drawn and murdered Tutt in cold blood before the latter even had time to clear leather. To the contrary, testified Hickok's defenders. Tutt went for his gun first and fired at the same time as Hickok. Most witnesses in the case swore they heard two shots, and the defense produced Tutt's gun with an empty chamber as evidence.

The next day a verdict was reached in the case of the *State of Missouri* v. *James B. Hickok* after a mere ten minutes of deliberation:

> Now at this day comes again the Circuit Attorney who prosecutes and the Defendant in person and by attorney and also the Jury heretofore imppannelled [*sic*] in this cause and having heard all the evidence introduced and the instructions of the Court upon their oath say "We the Jury find the Defendant not guilty in manner and form charged." It is therefore considered by the Court that the State take nothing by her suit, that the Defendant be discharged hereof and go hence without delay.

Predictably, the verdict was greeted with mixed reaction. The speedy decision of the jury suggests a prevailing sentiment in favor of self-defense; however, there were those who were quick to point out that the jury was composed entirely of Union men who were blinded by the loyalty issue. An anonymous writer for the 1883 *History of Greene County* claimed that when the verdict was announced, a prominent lawyer denounced it from the balcony of the court house, and some in the crowd threatened to lynch Bill, "but nothing was done."

Davis Tutt headstone at Maplewood Cemetery in Springfield.

Even the editor of the *Missouri Weekly Patriot* changed his tune once he heard the verdict. Whereas he had lauded Hickok for his exemplary military record two weeks earlier, in the August 10 edition of the paper, he noted the "general dissatisfaction felt by the citizens of this place with the verdict." In addition, he implied there was no logical reason to find Hickok innocent by reason of self-defense, because Wild Bill not only made no attempt to avoid the conflict with Tutt, but he actually initiated the shootout. The editor concluded wistfully, "The jury seems to have thought differently."

About a month after Hickok's acquittal, Col. George Ward Nichols arrived in Springfield to pen a romanticized version of the Tutt shootout and Wild Bill's other escapades for *Harper's New Monthly Magazine.* Hickok, meanwhile, hung around Springfield another five months or so. After testifying as an eyewitness in a murder case in January of 1866, he was summoned to Fort Riley, Kansas, where he was appointed a deputy United States marshal and made the acquaintance of George Armstrong Custer. When Nichols's article finally appeared in February of 1867, Wild Bill Hickok became a legend in his own time. His adventures over the next nine years, as he tried to live up to his reputation, only embellished the legend more. By the time Jack McCall shot him in the back of the head in Deadwood, South Dakota Territory, in August of 1876, Wild Bill was the most-famous figure in the American West.

2

The Rule of the Regulators

Three "Regulators" lurked in the dull light of dawn behind Green B. Phillips's barn in Greene County, Missouri, as the farmer and former Union captain trudged from his home near Cave Springs to begin his chores on the morning of May 23, 1866. Phillips went inside a nearby crib, where he started husking corn to feed his livestock. With revolvers drawn, the trespassers surrounded the unsuspecting farmer and poked the barrels of their pistols through the cracks and between the logs of the crib. While two of the men kept him covered, the third went to the door and ordered Phillips out.

When he complied, two of the men each gripped one of his arms and started herding him toward a gate leading to some timber while the third man walked behind him as a guard. The men had gone only about twenty feet when the powerful Phillips broke loose and made a dash for safety. He ran about thirty feet before stumbling over a hog that happened to be lying in his path. As Phillips tried to scramble to his feet, the assassins opened fire.

The Civil War had ripped the social fabric of the nation apart, and lawlessness abounded in many parts of the country in the months that followed. Nowhere was this truer than in the border state of Missouri, where sharply divided loyalties had given rise to a particularly vicious brand of guerrilla conflict during the war. Bushwhacking gangs, although mainly sympathetic to the Confederate cause, sometimes used the war as an excuse for mere plunder, preying on Southern and Northern victims alike.

A year after the war's end, it was clear to many citizens in the state that the armistice had not stopped the banditry. An organized gang of thieves centered on Walnut Grove in northwest Greene County seemed to be operating throughout southwest Missouri. Rarely were the brigands caught, and even when they were arrested and brought to trial, they often won acquittal with ready alibis backed by the testimony of cohorts or through intimidation of potential witnesses and jurymen.

A group of citizens in the Walnut Grove vicinity decided to take matters into their own hands. In the spring of 1866, they formed the Regulators for the express purpose of wiping out the nest of outlaws. (The faction may have taken its name from a vigilante group by the same designation that was briefly active fifty years earlier during Missouri's territorial days.) According to the 1883 *History of Greene County*, the Honest Man's League, as the group was sometimes called, was composed of "some of the best citizens" of the county.

Green Phillips was their first victim. Captain Phillips had served in the Enrolled Missouri Militia during the war. His unit had played an important role in the Union defense of Springfield during the Confederate invasion of Missouri in early 1863. Many who knew him considered the captain a solid citizen, but he had apparently brought suspicion upon himself by befriending the wrong people. One night around May 21 or 22, the Regulators met in a secret session, pronounced a death sentence on Phillips, and dispatched the three gunmen to carry it out. Now he lay dead, shot full of bullets in his own barnyard.

On Saturday, the twenty-sixth, three days after the murder, two young men, John Rush and Charles Gorsuch, went to Walnut Grove and openly condemned the shooting of Phillips. They then threatened two of the Regulators, whom they claimed were the killers. The vigilante group happened to be meeting that very day at the Rice schoolhouse just northeast of Walnut Grove, and news of the two men's presence in town and the substance of their threats were quickly carried to the conference. Rush and Gorsuch were impugned as members of the outlaw gang, and a summary trial was held. A "jury" of Regulators promptly passed a sentence of death on the two men and then set off at a gallop

Early-day Springfield square, similar to how it appeared when the Regulators occupied it. (Courtesy the History Museum for Springfield-Greene County)

toward Walnut Grove to carry it out. The leaguers entered the town from four directions and apprehended Rush and Gorsuch at a store. The Regulators took their captives about a mile southwest of the village, where, according to the county history, they were strung up to a redbud tree and soon "their dead bodies swung and swayed in the soft May breezes."

Two days later, on May 28, the Honest Man's League assembled in the Walnut Grove area, 250 strong, and rode seventeen miles to the county seat at Springfield. The Regulators galloped into the public square and lined up in a box formation in front of the courthouse. One of them, a Cumberland Presbyterian minister named George W. Brown, mounted a wagon that had been drawn up to serve as a makeshift rostrum and began to address the gathering crowd. Parson Brown told the people why the organization had been formed and what it had done in recent days. He declared that if possible, the Regulators meant to rid the county of thieves by legal means; however, if necessary, they would carry out justice upon the guilty in their own way. When the preacher relinquished the platform, another member of the Honest Man's League, Maj. L. P. Downing, rose to harangue the crowd along the same lines.

Then the Regulators invited some of the prominent citizens of Springfield to share their thoughts on the vigilante group and its activities. Col. James H. Baker, a Springfield lawyer and later a State Supreme Court justice, took the stand and sympathized with the organization. Although he lamented the necessity of the group's formation and urged the men to act within the law if possible, he vouched for the character of many of the Regulators and affirmed the righteousness of their motives. State senator J. W. D. L. F. Mack, known as "Alphabet" Mack, seconded Baker's remarks. However, the third speaker, former Missouri secretary of state John M. Richardson, looked upon the group with less favor, and he condemned its recent actions. The final speaker, U. S. congressman John S. Phelps, censured the group at some length. Phelps, who later served as governor of Missouri, suggested the actions already taken should be sufficient to send a clear signal to outlaws that thievery would not be tolerated in Greene County, and he urged the Regulators to refrain from further vigilantism. If the current laws were insufficient, Phelps claimed, they could be changed, and if the current elected officers were ineffective in carrying out the laws, they could be replaced.

After listening to the speakers, however, the editor of the *Springfield Weekly Patriot* said, "We do not believe that the law or the officers are at fault." The editor went on to say that the Civil War had left the country infested with such a large number of outlaws that it was virtually impossible to bring them to justice by normal means, and he suggested that "the unusual state of things required an extraordinary effort on the part of the honest portion of the community to remedy the evil and punish those guilty of crimes." Rival editor J. West Goodwin of the *Springfield Southwest Union Press* shared his competitor's favorable impression of the Regulators, remarking, "Their deportment, while in the city, was all that could be desired, each one attending to his own business and letting bad whisky alone."

John S. Phelps, who addressed the Regulators on the Springfield square. (Courtesy Wikimedia Commons)

Apparently the Regulators, like the editors, were unconvinced by Mr. Phelps's arguments. With shouts of "On to Ozark," they rode south out of Springfield toward Christian County and took possession of the county seat. From Ozark, they had marched out on the Forsyth road about two miles when they came upon James "Boss" Edwards, a fugitive from Greene County charged with theft, and took him prisoner. They tried him on the spot, found him guilty, and hanged him from a huge oak tree beside the road.

Although the Regulators had lynched Edwards in defiance of Phelps's appeal to work within the law, they shortly afterwards began an indifferent effort to cooperate with authorities. On June 6, they helped Deputy Sheriff Isaac Jones apprehend seven men in the Walnut Grove area. The men were charged with theft and jailed, but some of them were soon bailed out. This infuriated the Regulators, to whom legal maneuvering like bail bonds, changes of venue, and continuances were so much nonsense.

They decided that more direct action was once again called for, and on June 16, from Walnut Grove, they issued the following proclamation to the citizens of southwest Missouri:

> We, the Regulators, organized to assist in the enforcement of the civil law, and to put down an extensive thieving organization, known to exist in our midst, having succeeded in arresting and commuting to jail a number of persons charged with grand larceny, robbing and general lawlessness, whom we believe to be bad men, and finding several of them have been bailed out, thereby extending to them all opportunity of again putting into execution their diabolical purposes of robbing,

plundering and murdering their neighbors; therefore, we
hereby give notice that all persons bailing such parties out of
jail will be regarded as in sympathy if not in full cooperation
with such, and will be held strictly responsible for the conduct
and personal appearance at court for trial of all persons thus
bailed out of jail.

Emphatically by the Regulators

On July 28, 1866, the Regulators assembled for a mass
meeting at Cave Springs, a small village southeast of Walnut
Grove. The group elected the following officers: president, Dr.
A. C. Sloan; vice presidents, Elisha Dorsey and John Evans; and
secretaries, T. W. Coltrain and L. P. Downing (one of the men
who spoke at Springfield). On the motion of Parson Brown
(the other Springfield orator), the group drafted a series
of twelve resolutions justifying the organization, detailing
its purpose and procedures, and otherwise "expressing the
sentiments of the meeting," as a letter to the *Southwest Union
Press* from one of the group's members said at the time.

This organizational meeting, however, was one of the last acts
of the Regulators, because the group had been so effective as
to make its continued existence unnecessary. The murder of
one man whose only known guilt was by association and the
lynching of three others accused of theft had quickly gotten the
group's message across, and it dissolved about as fast as it had
sprung up. As Jonathan Fairbanks and Clyde Tuck observed
in their 1915 book *Past and Present of Greene County*, the Honest
Man's League had "struck terror into the hearts of the thieving
element, and very quickly rendered Greene County as free from
depredations . . . as any spot in any state could be."

Although the Regulators had taken the law into their own
hands, none of them were charged with any crime, because
they were widely viewed as "good men" and their victims as
"bad men." Despite the admonitions of men such as John S.
Phelps, the vigilante deeds of the Honest Man's League had
the implicit, if not the official, approval of county authorities
and the blessing of most area citizens.

In fact, for many years afterwards, the name of the

Regulators was often invoked around Greene County with a sort of wistful admiration any time a particularly evil crime was committed. "More than once," according to Fairbanks and Tuck, "men have been heard to wish that the old 'Honest Men's League' was still in existence to mete out swift and terrible justice to the criminals." Throughout the past one hundred years, though, memory of the Regulators has faded into obscurity to the point that their story is scarcely a footnote in the local lore.

3

Murdered for Preaching the Gospel?

Divided and embittered by four years of bloody conflict, citizens of the border state of Missouri nursed their rancor long after treaties officially ended the Civil War in the spring of 1865. Old resentments died hard, and outbreaks of violence spawned by the lingering animosity plagued the state for years.

One such atrocity was the murder of Rev. S. S. Headlee in Webster County on July 28, 1866. The *Springfield Southwest Union,* in reporting the incident a week later, said Headlee had been slain for preaching the gospel. However, it was not as simple as that.

Samuel S. Headlee, a native of Tennessee, had come to Missouri at a young age with his parents. He was received into the ministry of the Methodist Episcopal Church South in 1852, spent the years leading up to the war assigned to the Springfield District of the St. Louis Conference, and often preached at Pleasant View Church just across the Greene County line in northwest Webster County.

The coming of the Civil War split the church along political lines, and some members of the congregation eventually defected to the M. E. Church North. Reverend Headlee alienated Unionists in the area with his outspoken support of the South, but one particularly audacious act aroused their special ire. In December of 1861, Reverend Headlee took a club and knocked down a U. S. flag the Union men had erected at Pleasant View Church. "If it has any friends," Headlee challenged, "let them take care of it."

No one accepted the dare at the time, as Southern sentiment was still prevalent among the congregation, at least on this day. News of Headlee's deed was quickly carried to Springfield, where it was cheered by the Missouri State

A cemetery is all that remains to mark the spot of the old Pleasant View Church.

Guard troops of Gen. Sterling Price, encamped in the city at the time. Loyalists later alleged also that men acting in concert with Reverend Headlee hunted down and tormented some of the Unionists who had raised the U. S. flag.

The tide turned, of course, and both Union force and Union sentiment eventually dominated in the Greene County area. Toward the end of the war, members of the Methodist Church North took over the building at Pleasant View, which the Southern church had built and still claimed title to. They made improvements to the church building and were in possession of it when the war ended.

Union might and Union feeling ultimately prevailed (to a lesser degree) in Missouri as a whole. In April of 1865, the state convention adopted a new constitution, called the Drake Constitution after its chief legislative proponent, that prohibited anyone who had ever supported the Confederate cause from voting or holding office and from teaching, preaching, practicing law, or engaging in certain other occupations. Anyone wishing to engage in these activities was required to sign a loyalty oath. In what to Southern

The "New" Pleasant View Church, about a mile from the site of the old one.

sympathizers must have been a bitter paradox, they were even forbidden from voting on ratification of these disenfranchising stipulations. With unrepentant Southerners excluded from the ballot, the Drake Constitution passed by only a very narrow margin in June of 1865 when it was put to a statewide vote. (It passed overwhelmingly in Greene County.)

Reverend Headlee refused to take the loyalty oath, but he remained relatively silent until the Reverend D. R. McAnally, editor of the *St. Louis Christian Advocate* and a leader in the M. E. Church South, summoned him to St. Louis about a year after the war's close. Following his conference with McAnally and other church leaders, Reverend Headlee, as presiding elder of the Springfield District, came back to the Greene County area determined to preach the gospel and try to restore the Methodist congregations that had been torn asunder by the Civil War to the M. E. Church South.

Around July 1, 1866, he spoke at Pleasant View in the presence of both supporters and detractors. One of the latter was the Reverend Henderson McNabb. Although he had formerly been a member of the M. E. Church South and had allegedly ordered a preacher to leave Pleasant View Church a few years earlier because of the minister's abolitionist views, McNabb had switched his allegiance to the Northern Methodists and was now the leader of the group who had taken possession of the Pleasant View Church. When Headlee announced his intention to hold a two-day revival and organizational meeting at Pleasant View beginning on the twenty-eighth of the month, McNabb turned to one of Headlee's supporters. "You will not hold that meeting," McNabb warned.

Then, as Headlee was leaving the grounds after his speech, one of McNabb's allies remarked in a voice loud enough for those around him to hear, "Somebody had better be preparing to die."

McNabb and his closest followers drew up a remonstrance opposing Headlee's scheduled appearance at the church, and they gathered the signatures of twenty-eight men from the surrounding area. The document was made known to the public and to Reverend Headlee in particular, but he remained determined to keep his appointment at the church.

On Friday, July 27, the day before Headlee's scheduled meeting, McNabb went about the neighborhood organizing a group of men to stop Headlee from preaching. At the church the next morning, one man in the gathering mob threatened to hang or shoot Headlee if he came on the grounds, and others expressed agreement with the sentiment. Friends of Headlee who had also gathered at the church sent word that perhaps he had better cancel his appearance, but they could not dissuade him. (Curiously, the Regulators, the subject of the previous chapter, held a mass meeting in northwest Greene County on this very same day, but there's no evidence to suggest that any of McNabb's allies were members of the Honest Man's League.)

Shortly before noon, Headlee arrived as scheduled at the Pleasant View Church and was met by Henderson McNabb and an angry crowd of twenty men. Headlee told McNabb that he understood the mob meant to hang or shoot him. In response, McNabb simply repeated his warning that Headlee had better not attempt to preach. Headlee asked by what authority McNabb was acting in preventing him from preaching at a church that Headlee and his followers had helped build and to which the M. E. Church South still held title. McNabb gestured toward the gang of men gathered outside the church. "There is my authority."

Headlee read from documents concerning church discipline to show his right to preach at Pleasant View, but McNabb told him that he and his friends had forfeited their rights by their treason and rebellion. Headlee said he knew he was preaching without having taken the oath prescribed by the new constitution and that he was willing to answer to the law for that. McNabb replied that he didn't care for the law and again told Headlee that he wasn't going to preach at the church.

Headlee, who knew most of the men in the mob, tried to reason with them, but they simply hurled abuse at him. One of them shouted, "Andy Johnson pardons rebels, but we don't; we put them through."

Another, after consulting with a few of his cohorts, stepped forward and said, "Mr. Headlee, we have heard enough from you. It is time for you to leave."

A sketch drawn by Nic Frising depicting the murder of Samuel S. Headlee.

Headlee realized his arguments were futile. Alarmed by the hostility of the mob, he appealed to McNabb for protection, and McNabb told him that if he would leave and never return he would not be harmed. Headlee, who owned property a half-mile south of the church, then asked if he could go preach on his own land.

"Yes," McNabb replied, "you may preach to your own rebel brethren on your own land as much as you please."

Headlee asked whether he would be followed, and McNabb assured him that he would not be. Headlee and his few supporters prepared to leave, but as Headlee started toward his horse, some of the mob shoved the barrels of their guns against him, cursing him and pushing him forward. "Let me alone," Headlee said. "I can walk without help."

The gang momentarily backed off, but Headlee and his small group had gone only about a quarter of a mile when four men who had been among the mob at the church came galloping up. One of them, William Drake, drew his revolver and, cursing Headlee, demanded to know whether he was sorry he had knocked down the U. S. flag at the start of the war. (Drake was likely one of the men who had erected it. The *Springfield Weekly Missouri Patriot* suggested as much in reporting the murder, and Headlee stated on his deathbed that he knew he was going to die as soon as he saw Drake ride up.)

"Talk to me like a gentleman," Headlee replied, "and I'll talk to you."

The young man repeated the question several times, punctuating it with more insults. When Headlee refused to answer, Drake shot him three times, twice through the body and once through the flesh of the hip. Then the assailant and his three buddies turned and galloped back to McNabb's house, where the rest of the mob had retreated after the confrontation at the church.

The mortally wounded Headlee rode on for about fifty yards before alighting from his horse and remarking calmly to his small band of followers, "Friends, I am a dead man." He was taken to his sister's house half a mile away, where he suffered throughout the day. His wife was summoned from the couple's home about thirteen miles away. His only brother showed up about nine o'clock that night when Reverend Headlee was "wading deep in the cold Jordan of death." An hour later, he expressed his final words of endearment to his wife and kids, asked the Lord's mercy on the men responsible for his death, and then died an agonizing death. His body was taken back to his home south of Fair Grove and buried at Elm Springs Cemetery.

News of the murder set off a war of words between the Southern-leaning *Springfield Southwest Union Press* and the rival *Springfield Weekly Missouri Patriot*. The *Press* called Headlee's killing a cold-blooded murder and captioned its story of the incident with the following subhead: "His Crime: Preaching the Gospel." The *Patriot*, on the other hand, stated, "The man who shot Mr. Headlee is not the only one to blame for his death" and went on to suggest that the Reverend McAnally and others who encouraged Headlee to preach in defiance of the law (i.e. the Drake Constitution) must share in the guilt. In the same issue, the *Patriot* also published a letter from Reverend McNabb, who defended his actions and claimed not to know who had shot Headlee.

Headlee's friends and colleagues throughout the state clamored for justice, but they got little satisfaction. Finally, four years after the murder, McNabb was indicted in Webster County for the crime but was acquitted upon his trial at Hartville. About the same time, William Drake was also arrested and charged in the murder, but he, too, was acquitted.

It was another ten years before the divisive passions of the Civil War had cooled enough that observers could discuss Headlee's death with any degree of detachment. In 1883, R. I. Holcombe, editor and principal author of the *History of Greene County*, in discussing the circumstances surrounding Headlee's killing and the feud between Southern and Northern Methodists that gave rise to it, offered a wry perspective that is still apt 125 years later. "That was the way," Holcombe concluded, "the brethren and followers of the meek and lowly Jesus dwelt together in unity in those days of the reconstruction period."

4

Troublous Times in the
Cherokee Neutral Lands

On the morning of February 10, 1869, a mob of settlers
stormed into Baxter Springs, Kansas, from the surrounding
Cherokee Neutral Lands, intent on closing down the land
office of the Missouri River, Fort Scott & Gulf Railroad that
had recently opened in the town. Part of the group took
over the vacant office, while another squad went in search
of the agents in charge of the office, John T. Cox and W.
B. Shockley. Locating the pair at a local hotel, the settlers
arrested them and marched them back to the land office,
where they threatened to hang Cox if he didn't turn over the
railroad's official papers within ten minutes.

Both Cox and Shockley claimed not to know the
combination of the safe in which the papers were locked.
The ensuing delay gave Cherokee County sheriff William
G. Seright time to assemble some of the town's citizens,
including newspaper editor M. W. Coulter, to resist the mob
and protect the railroad papers. Confronted by the hastily
formed posse, the settlers held a consultation and decided to
depart peaceably, but the land office was shortly afterwards
abandoned because of threats and intimidation from the
railroad's enemies.

The altercation in Baxter Springs was just the beginning
of what would prove to be the biggest railroad-settler dispute
in Kansas history. Revolving around the conflicting claims of
the settlers and the railroad to the Cherokee Neutral Lands,
the quarrel had been building for months, but now it had
erupted into open hostility.

Located in the southeast corner of Kansas, the Neutral Lands
were originally set aside to serve as a buffer between Osage
Indians and Missouri settlers after terms of the Osage Treaty
of 1825 removed the Osages from Missouri and relocated

Missouri River, Fort Scott & Gulf Railroad (now renamed) as it appears today.

them on the Kansas plains. Covering approximately 800,000 acres, the lands encompassed an area about twenty-five miles wide (east to west) and fifty miles long (north to south) and comprised what later become Cherokee County, Crawford County, and an eight-mile strip of southern Bourbon County.

When the Cherokee Indians were removed from Georgia under terms of the 1835 Treaty of New Echota, the Neutral Lands were ceded to the Cherokees for a half-million dollars as an addition to their main reservation in nearby Indian Territory (now Oklahoma), and the Neutral Lands became known as the Cherokee Neutral Lands. However, few members of the tribe actually occupied the area. So, when white settlers began squatting on the lands shortly before, during, and immediately after the Civil War, the Cherokees decided to sell the tract, and in August of 1866, they signed a treaty ceding the Neutral Lands in trust to the United States government to act as their agent in completing the transaction.

Secretary of the Interior James Harlan sold the lands on August 30, 1866, to the American Emigrant Company. But Harlan's successor, Orville H. Browning, set aside the contract on the opinion of the U. S. attorney general that the purchase was void because it did not involve a lump-sum cash payment as stipulated in the treaty but instead was made on time. Settlers on the Neutral Lands implored their Kansas representatives in the U. S. Congress to use their influence to prevent another sale of the land, but despite pledges to help from both Sen. Samuel C. Pomeroy and Congressman Sidney Clarke, Browning sold the land on October 9, 1867, to James F. Joy for $800,000. Considered the "Railway King of the Northwest," Joy was president of the Michigan Central Railroad and had interests in several other railroads. In the Neutral Lands purchase, he was representing the Missouri River, Fort Scott & Gulf Railroad (sometimes called the Border Tier Railroad), which planned to build a road from Kansas City to Baxter Springs through the eastern edge of Kansas.

The settlers immediately questioned the validity of the Joy purchase. Moreover, the American Emigrant Company had not relinquished its claim to the lands. However, the latter conflict was settled by a supplemental treaty in April of 1868 that basically set aside the Joy sale but assigned the American Emigrant Company's interest to Joy. Congress ratified the supplemental treaty on June 6, 1868, and the president proclaimed it on June 10.

Dissatisfaction with Joy's acquisition of the land grew throughout the summer and fall of that year, but the settlers continued expressing their opposition primarily through legal means. They sought redress through their elected representatives in the Kansas legislature and the U. S. Congress, and they sent William R. Laughlin, an area farmer and aspiring politician, to Washington, D. C., to lobby on their behalf. They also began forming "Land Leagues," organized by township, then by county, and governed by an overall committee called the Central Land League, to resist the railroad. That the sentiment of the settlers largely predominated in local politics is illustrated by the fact that the president of the Central Land League, C. C. McDowell, was elected a representative to the Kansas State Legislature in the fall elections of 1868.

Both opponents and proponents of the railroad held mass meetings at Baxter Springs, Columbus, Fort Scott, Girard, and other area towns, and representatives of the two sides fired off impassioned letters that were published in local and regional newspapers. Both sides used various legal arguments to advance their cause. One of the settlers' contentions, for example, was that the Cherokee Indians had forfeited their claim to the lands by their alliance with the Confederacy during the Civil War and that Joy's purchase of the lands from the Indians was, therefore, null and void. Supporters of the railroad, on the other hand, insisted that the Cherokees were the rightful owners of the land, that the government had acted only as an agent in the transaction between them and Joy, and that, therefore, the squatters had had no right to settle on the lands to begin with.

The dispute became more heated when Joy opened a "Cherokee Neutral Land Office" in Fort Scott in early December and had a circular printed giving notice to settlers living on the land that they had until the following April to make entry of or "prove up" their claims and thereby prevent the sale of their lands to other purchasers. Under the terms outlined by Joy, residents who had settled on the land prior to June 10, 1868, the date of the supplemental treaty that ratified his purchase, would be required to pay from $1.50 to $4.00 an acre for their land (depending on such factors as its proximity to the proposed railroad). Those who had settled after June 10 and any subsequent newcomers would have to pay from $2.00 to $5.00 an acre. The established settlers, however, felt they should be entitled to their lands free or, at worst, be allowed to purchase them for $1.25 an acre under the homestead or preemption laws. Proponents of the railroad countered that the Neutral Lands had not been in the public domain since 1835, when they were ceded to the Cherokees, and that the territory was not subject to the homestead or preemption laws.

The quarrel grew even more heated in January of 1869 when survey parties for the railroad began moving into the Neutral Lands. A month later, the conflict had escalated to open confrontation with the settlers' attempt to shut down the land office at Baxter Springs. It would soon explode into violence.

A series of resolutions adopted by the anti-Joy league of Lincoln Township and Crawford County and published in area newspapers about the same time as the raid on the Baxter Springs land office serves to illustrate the animus that settlers harbored toward the railroad. The resolutions stated that if John T. Cox attempted to open a land office in Crawford County, it would be deemed a public nuisance and settlers would be within their rights to "abate such a nuisance; peaceably if we can—forcibly if we must." The document went on to say that anyone who assisted or sympathized with Cox in the establishment of such a land office would have the same treatment meted out to him as was proposed for Cox. Also, any settler who "proved up" under the Joy contract would be hanged "higher than Haman, and without benefit of clergy." The proclamation concluded by stating that the settlers "mean action" and would "make an example of the first person who violates any of said resolutions." W. G. Cunningham, J. S. Armsworthy, and W. G. Clark signed the document.

An even bigger stronghold of anti-Joy sentiment than Lincoln Township was Columbus, the county seat of Cherokee County. When agent J. W. Davis tried to open a land office there in April of 1869, he was ordered to leave town, and, according to a Kansas historian, "it was a mandate he lost no time obeying."

On Saturday, April 24, 1869, state senator M. V. Voss ventured to Columbus to address a gathering of about 175 settlers concerning the Neutral Lands question. Voss had said he opposed the general idea of large-scale sales of land to single individuals such as in the case at hand. However, he felt open opposition to the railroad was foolish, had suggested that the dispute be settled in the courts, and had recently given a speech condemning secret land leagues. His middle-of-the-road stance apparently had not earned him any points among the anti-Joy crowd. When he arrived and prepared to speak, some of the crowd began throwing rocks at him, and he promptly got back in his buggy. As he started off, two or three shots were fired into the air, but Voss made a "masterly retreat in good order" to Baxter Springs. His speech there two days later to a prorailroad audience was more warmly received, although it was reported by at least one newspaper that the leaguers tried to disrupt this meeting as well.

A few days later, on April 30, angry settlers accosted a survey crew under J. A. J. Chapman and John Runk, Jr., engineers for the railroad, and took the two men and their workers prisoner. After burning the crew's wagons, tents, surveying instruments, and other supplies, the settlers drove the subordinate workers from the Neutral Lands with orders never to return to employment of the railroad, under penalty of death. They then took Chapman and Runk several miles south, stripped off their coats, blindfolded them, gave them fifteen lashes with a whip, and told them to leave the Neutral Lands and not say anything about what had happened or they would be killed.

A few days after the assault on the survey party, settlers burned about a thousand railroad ties near Cow Creek in Cherokee County. The total number of ties destroyed in Cherokee County throughout the spring and summer of 1869 was later reported by antileaguers as 26,000, but this was probably a bit of hyperbole, as both sides tended to exaggerate the malicious deeds of the other.

The dispute between the settlers and the railroad became so contentious in the late spring of 1869 that Kansas governor James M. Harvey issued a proclamation on May 31. He enjoined the people of Cherokee and Crawford counties "to yield due obedience to the officers of the law, to cease all acts of violence and lawlessness and to look to the properly constituted authorities for the redress of grievances and the determination of legal rights." At the same time, he applied to the U. S. government to send federal troops to the Neutral Lands to help maintain order, but the prospect of their arrival hardly checked the increasing intimidation and violence.

During May and June, settlers who chose to prove their

claims under the Joy contract or who otherwise opposed the settlers' leagues were regularly forced off their land, often taking refuge in Fort Scott. One such settler was A. V. Peters, who was driven from his farm in Spring Valley Township of Cherokee County around the end of May. On June 2, William Hayhurst of the Spring Valley Settlers' League sent Peters a letter inviting him to return if he would sign a pledge to "refrain from speaking, acting, writing or otherwise operating against the league." Peters declined the invitation and, instead, turned the letter over to a Fort Scott newspaper.

Particularly active in the intimidation of Joy settlers was a squad of men near the small village of Wirtonia led by a farmer and itinerant Methodist minister named Vincent. He reportedly made a fiery speech in which he said he would "fight Joy until hell froze over, and then fight it out on the ice."

The clash between leaguers and antileaguers turned deadly when Jeremiah Murphy, a zealous leaguer, started for his home from Columbus around noon on Sunday, June 6, 1869. Later in the day, he was found dead about two miles from town, having received a bullet through each eye and another through the nose, "completely tearing his head to pieces." Coulter, editor of the *Cherokee (Baxter Springs) Sentinel,* dismissed the incident: "Mr. Murphy was known to be a rampant Leaguer, and, we presume, had taken a very active part in driving peaceful, law-abiding citizens from their homes." The prorailroad *Fort Scott Monitor* justified the murder by quoting a passage of Scripture: "Whoso sheddeth man's blood, by man shall his blood be shed."

The *Sentinel* reported at the time of the murder that there was no clue as to who had committed it, but Amos Sanford, probate judge of Cherokee County and an outspoken defender of the settlers' leagues, later claimed that the murderer was a white man disguised as an Indian who had been traced to Baxter Springs.

The first company of Federal troops reached the Neutral Lands around the middle of June and were stationed at Crawfordsville, a small town about two or three miles west of

Girard. Their presence, however, did not immediately deter the leaguers, at least partly because the settlers were kept stirred up by politicians who championed their cause. For example, Congressman Clarke, in a speech at Iowa City, Crawford County, on July 8, 1869, told settlers he did not advise violence against the railroad but that if they stood firm and united, no road would ever be built. "Why?" he asked rhetorically.

Because if a weary traveler should come along, and wishing to rest, sit down upon a pile of railroad ties, and, while smoking his pipe, a spark should happen to fall and burn up the ties, could any one blame you for it, and say that you were using violence to prevent the construction of the road? I reckon not. . . . I don't advise force to prevent this most damnable railroad swindle, but I know that these accidents do and will happen in the best regulated communities. Now, gentlemen, if any such thing should happen to this swindling road, you must all be in bed and asleep when it happens, or as soon after as possible.

The settlers must have gotten the not-too-subtle message, because "the speaker was scarcely off the Neutral Lands" when a party of settlers went to the assessor's house in Osage Township, put him under guard, and took the abstract of lands owned by the railroad in order to prevent the assessment of the lands. A similar attempt was made in Baker Township, but the abstract could not be located. Then, on July 17, a mob of settlers attacked the workmen on the railroad in southern Bourbon County near the Crawford County line and destroyed all the tents and tools of the workers.

At least partly because of the presence of the Federal troops, open acts of violence gradually subsided during the late summer and fall of 1869, but the dispute between settlers and the railroad continued to be argued in the court of public opinion. In October, Judge Sanford started a newspaper at Columbus called the *Workingman's Journal*. In virtually every issue, he railed against the railroad "monopolists" and the "eastern capitalists."

In November, William Warner, publisher and editor of the pro-Joy *Fort Scott Press,* moved his newspaper, under the aegis of the railroad, to Girard, where it became the *Girard Press.* Warner and Coulter, editor of the *Cherokee Sentinel,* countered Sanford's radical prosettler stance with regular denunciations of the exploits of the "bloody leaguers."

Sanford found his most strident voice in early December after he was, according to his own account, "publicly cow-hided on the streets" of the "so-called city" of Bax-ter Springs. The man who administered the lashing was Benjamin F. Evans, whom

U. S. congressman Sidney Clarke lobbied on behalf of the settlers opposing the railroad. (Courtesy Research Division of the Oklahoma Historical Society)

Sanford called a "non-working man" and a "miserable Missouri puke, who has not been known to have performed a day's work for the last six months." Sanford claimed the incident happened in full view of and with the tacit approval of Baxter's leading citizens, a charge that Coulter did not dispute in the following week's *Sentinel.* In fact, Coulter largely defended the whipping by intimating that Sanford deserved to be flogged because of his rabble-rousing and supposed verbal abuse of Evans a few weeks earlier in Columbus (a claim Sanford denied).

Even as the leaguers and their supporters like Sanford continued to rage against the railroad in public, some of them began secretly proving up their claims under the Joy contract. By 1870, the conflict between leaguers and antileaguers was reduced to occasional instances of intimidation, such as the one that occurred at Checo, a small community a few miles northeast of Baxter Springs, in mid January. H. M. Tremble, a preacher and businessman from Baxter Springs, stopped at the community on January 10 to spend the evening with a friend and was invited by his host to preach at a divine service being held in a local schoolhouse. Tremble hesitated at first, because he was engaged in providing crossties to the Missouri River, Fort Scott & Gulf Railroad, and he knew that most of his audience were leaguers, but he finally accepted the offer. When he rose to speak, however, a commotion broke out at the back of the room, and Tremble's friend hastily informed him that he had better not preach after all or else "there would be great trouble." According to Tremble, he "did not feel like yielding to the gag law," but he declined to preach because of his friend's earnest supplication.

The settlers, of course, resented the presence of the Federal troops and had suggested almost from the time they arrived that they should be withdrawn. In February of 1870, a committee of the state legislature visited the Neutral Lands to determine the necessity of maintaining the troops there. A majority of the committee concluded that the soldiers should stay until the land dispute was settled in the courts.

The Missouri River, Fort Scott & Gulf Railroad reached its terminus at Baxter Springs in early May of 1870. Joy's original plan, as the name of the railroad indicated, was for the road to go all the way to Texas, and the Cherokee Indians, who owned most of the territory through which the road would have to pass, had granted a right of way. Partly because of the delay created by the difficulties with the settlers, however, Baxter Springs was as far as the tracks got. By the time Joy's railroad reached Baxter, the rival Katy (Missouri-Kansas-Texas) Railroad had already reached Chetopa, located twenty miles west of Baxter, and the government had previously stipulated that whichever railroad reached Kansas's southern border first would be the one that could build through Indian Territory. Backers of the Missouri River, Fort Scott & Gulf encountered a further difficulty when they learned that, unlike the Cherokees, the Quapaw tribe, which owned a narrow ribbon of land below Baxter Springs called the Quapaw Strip, had not granted a right of way.

In May of 1871, the district court finally rendered a ruling deciding the Neutral Lands dispute in favor of the railroad, but while the decision was being appealed to the Supreme Court, the dispute continued to erupt into sporadic acts of violence. One of the last such incidents occurred in July of 1871 when a party of settlers burned the office of the *Girard Press* because Warner, at least in the opinion of the leaguers, was little more than a mouthpiece for James Joy.

The Federal troops, who occupied the Neutral Lands ostensibly to keep order, instigated a few disturbances of their own. In September of 1871, some troops of the Seventh Cavalry destroyed a large amount of property at Chetopa, and shortly afterwards some boisterous soldiers were locked up at Columbus for their raucous antics and ended up exchanging gunfire with local police when friends broke them out of jail. Incidents such as these merely deepened the resentment that the settlers felt toward the Federal troops.

In November of 1872, the Supreme Court upheld the opinion of the lower court in favor of the railroad, and most of the settlers who had not already bought their lands through Joy promptly did so after this decision. Then, in February of 1873, the Federal troops withdrew.

Although the anti-Joy leaguers had lost in the U. S. courts, they remained a major force in local politics for several years, supporting what was called the Settler's Ticket. Columbus, the stronghold of the settlers during the Neutral Lands dispute, became a hub of farm commerce, and it retains a distinctly rural flavor even today.

Baxter Springs, meanwhile, enjoyed a momentary boom as a Kansas cow town after the railroad arrived, but then it went into a period of economic decline. Although the town later recovered, its course during the late-nineteenth century, as well as that of surrounding towns, was shaped as much by Joy's loss in his race with the Katy Railroad as it was by his Pyrrhic victory in his fight with the settlers over the Neutral Lands.

5

The Killin' Killians

When William Norton gunned down Jake Killian on the streets of Empire City, Kansas, on March 28, 1878, the incident marked not just the end of a long-running feud between the two men, but also the climactic episode in what the nearby *Joplin (Missouri) Herald* called at the time "the remarkable history of a remarkable family." In the annals of southwest Missouri and surrounding area, the notorious Killian family had authored "a chapter of crimes and historical events" dating back to before the Civil War.

The Killian clan first came to public notice in the small lead-mining town of Granby, Missouri, shortly after migrating there from Carroll County, Arkansas, around 1854. The forty-five-year-old father, "old Cy Killian," reportedly spent most of his time and money in the "gin mills" of the mining camp and quickly earned a reputation as a "dangerous and quarrelsome man" because of his "many difficulties with his neighbors."

He tried to get work at a local mine and was refused because he was considered too old, but he succeeded in gaining employment for his three oldest sons: Benjamin, who was in his early twenties; Martin, who was in his late teens; and Jacob, who was about seventeen. The boys, though, gave their employers so much trouble "on account of their quarrelsome dispositions" that they were soon discharged. Later, Mart, the second son, gave it another try but "failed to give satisfaction" and was again let go.

On August 10, 1858, "old man" Killian and a drinking buddy named William Collins were on a spree together when they got into an argument in front of a grocery store, where Killian was seated on a bench. After a few heated words, Collins picked up a nearby whiffletree and beat Killian to death with it. Allowed to remain at large, Collins hung

Early-day Granby. (Courtesy Granby Miner's Museum)

around Granby for a couple of weeks and then took off never to be heard from again.

Not long after his father was killed, Mart Killian left Granby for parts unknown, and when he returned, he was missing one of his arms. He said he'd had it shot off while he was crossing the western plains.

Nevertheless, the disability didn't keep him from joining the army when the Civil War broke out. Toward the middle of the war, Mart and his unit, Company K of the Sixth Kansas Cavalry, were headed to Carthage, Missouri, from the north when he and a fellow soldier named Wentworth temporarily left the command and went into Lamar. While there, they got into a row with a saloonkeeper, and Killian supposedly ravished the man's wife. Then, after he and Wentworth caught up with their unit at Carthage, Killian robbed a man named Scruggs of two watches, for which he was arrested and tried by a drumhead court-martial. Killian was found guilty and was sentenced to have his head shaved, to be branded with a "T" for "thief" on his left hip, and to be confined in jail for thirty days with only bread and water to eat. After he was placed in jail, his unit left Carthage. A few days later, though, a detail was sent back to town to check on him. They found the jail broken into and the prisoner missing. They later learned Killian had been taken from the jail and hanged from a tree at nearby Spring River, supposedly by a party of bushwhackers from Lamar who had come to avenge the outrage on the saloonkeeper's wife.

Early in the war, Jake Killian was apparently involved in guerrilla activity on the side of the Confederacy or was at least a Southern sympathizer, because in February of 1863 at Newtonia, he was required to sign an oath of allegiance to the United States. Later he joined the Union Army, and, like his older brother, he, too, was unable to avoid trouble, even in the military. One day in 1864, he and William Norton, a fellow member of the Eighth Missouri Cavalry, quarreled over a game of cards in a cabin at Brownsville, Arkansas. Disputing the outcome of a hand that Norton had apparently won, Killian jumped up, grabbed the money, and kicked over the table. Norton also sprang to his feet, and both men drew their revolvers. In the struggle that followed, Killian got behind Norton and put him in a bear hug, pinning his arms down, but Norton turned his revolver upward and fired over his right shoulder. The ball struck Killian in the face, destroying his sight in one eye. From that time forward, the two men became bitter enemies, but the war ended before Killian could exact the revenge he had sworn to take. Killian returned to Granby while Norton moved to Dallas County, Missouri, about ninety miles away, and the two men apparently lost track of each other.

On the evening of August 21, 1869, Jake Killian attended William Lake's traveling Hippo-Olympiad and Mammoth Circus, which was performing in Granby. While clearing out the big top after the main show and collecting tickets for the minstrel show that was to follow, ushers found Killian hidden under a seat. When one of the ushers told him to come out and either pay or leave, he stood up, sat down on a seat, and refused to move. Informed of the commotion, William Lake, owner of the circus, also ordered Killian out, but the trespasser still wouldn't leave. Lake then grabbed Killian by the collar and told his men to put him out. During the scuffle, Killian went for his revolver, but the ushers wrestled it away from him and herded him outside, where he reportedly told bystanders he would kill Lake as soon as he could get another gun.

Killian left but returned minutes later, telling the circus's doorkeeper that he was not a quarrelsome man and was willing to pay to get in. While he was paying, though, Lake approached, and Killian, seeing the circus owner, slipped back among the crowd at the door. About this time, a deputy marshal, having learned of the earlier disturbance, showed up, and he and a man named Thompson started talking to Lake. As they did so, Killian slipped up behind Thompson and the deputy, extended a revolver over Thompson's right shoulder, and shot Lake in the chest. During the panic that ensued, the gunman dashed away but tripped over a guy rope and fell on his face, accidentally discharging his revolver a second time. Recovering quickly, he jumped up and made his escape.

Meanwhile, Lake, after being shot, staggered a few yards and collapsed. "My God, boys!" he exclaimed. "I am killed. Carry me home." He was taken immediately to his nearby hotel room, where he died as soon as he arrived. He was buried at Granby two days later.

Lake's widow, Agnes (who later married Wild Bill Hickok), offered a reward of $1,000 for the capture of Killian, and the Granby Odd Fellows' lodge put up another $300. Killian remained at large for some time, however, until a man who had reportedly struck a bargain with the fugitive by which Killian was to share in the reward money finally brought him in. At Killian's first trial, the jury failed to reach a verdict, and the defendant took a change of venue from Newton to neighboring McDonald County, where the case was continued. Finally, another change of venue brought the trial back to Newton County, and Killian was convicted in February of 1874 and sentenced to a term of approximately four years in the state penitentiary.

While Jake Killian's case was being settled in the courts,

Agnes Lake Thatcher, widow of William Lake and later wife of Bill Hickok.
(Courtesy Kansas State Historical Society)

his oldest brother, Ben, was busy getting himself in trouble in much the same manner that Jake had. On the evening of August 15, 1873, Ben and a sidekick named Jim Hale got liquored up and went to the Hamilton, Blanchard, and Company's Indian Show, which was playing at Granby on the same grounds where Ben's younger brother had killed William Lake four years earlier. The two ruffians got into an squabble with a black man named Charley Thomas, drew their revolvers, and started firing. Thomas returned fire, and in the exchange of lead, an innocent bystander, Mathias Schmidt, was killed; Thomas was seriously wounded; and two female spectators received minor wounds.

Thomas was taken into custody, while Killian and Hale went about town "blustering and flourishing their pistols for an hour after the disturbance" without any attempt made to arrest them. Not until after they had left town was a posse finally organized to track them down. Although Hale made his escape, Killian was soon captured and brought back to Newton County.

Even though a large-caliber ball was taken from Schmidt's body and Killian reportedly had the only large-chambered pistol of the three men involved in the gunplay and even though Thomas was standing with his back to the circus spectators at the time of the shootout, Thomas was accused of being the one who fired the shot that killed Schmidt. He was found guilty and sentenced to a term of ten years in prison. Meanwhile, Ben Killian's case was postponed several times, and when the case finally did come to trial, he was acquitted for his part in the affray.

On August 25, 1875, eighteen-year-old Thomas Killian, not to be outdone by his older brothers, teamed up with two young men, John Wilson and John Humphreys, to kill John Anderson, an estimable citizen of Newton County who had been the foreman of the grand jury that indicted Ben Killian for the murder of Schmidt. When Tom was arrested in Arkansas two months later, he claimed Wilson and Humphreys, who was Killian's cousin, had robbed and deserted him and had done the shooting in the Anderson murder. Nonetheless, Tom was tried, convicted, and sentenced to ninety-nine years in the penitentiary for his part in the crime.

During the early part of 1877, some of Jake Killian's friends applied to have him released from the state prison on a plea of failing health, and he was set free on the three-fourths rule after serving slightly over three years of his term. Jake returned to the Newton County area, and upon learning that his old enemy William Norton was residing in neighboring

Jasper County, he renewed his threats of revenge and reportedly started stalking Norton.

William Norton, though, was not a man to be trifled with. In addition to having blinded Killian during the Civil War, Norton had since killed a man named John Murphy in Joplin, Missouri, and was rumored to have killed another, although both cases were said to be self defense. Some time after lead was discovered on Short Creek in the spring of 1877, he moved from Joplin to Empire City, where he opened a grocery store and went to work in the mines. But no matter where he went, he apparently maintained "a sharp lookout for his enemy, particularly when Jake was in the vicinity."

About March 26, 1878, Killian showed up on Short Creek, where one of his sisters lived, and started spreading the word around Empire City and the neighboring mining camp of Galena that he planned to kill Norton on sight. About three o'clock on the afternoon of March 28, after having gotten word of Killian's threats, Norton left his diggings at the edge of Empire City and went into town to retrieve a double-barreled shotgun and a revolver from his store. He had just stepped back into the street when he saw Killian come around the corner of a saloon. Norton raised his shotgun and, without a word, fired both barrels into the chest of the unarmed Killian, who immediately fell to the ground. Norton then stepped up to the body and pulled out his revolver. "Damn you, are you dead yet?" he exclaimed, as he fired a shot into the back of Killian's head.

Despite the seemingly cold-blooded circumstances of the killing, the overwhelming opinion on Short Creek and at neighboring Joplin favored Norton because of Killian's notorious reputation and the threats he had made against Norton. When a man who had testified on Norton's behalf at the coroner's inquest and who planned to testify at Norton's trial was found dead at the bottom of a mine shaft a week and a half later, friends of Killian were immediately suspected, and opinion congealed in favor of Norton. At his trial in early May, the jury returned a verdict of not guilty after deliberating only thirty minutes, thus bringing to a close the saga of Jake Killian and his remarkable family.

6

The Bloody Benders of Southeast Kansas

On the morning of March 10, 1873, Dr. William H. York left his parents' farm near Fort Scott, Kansas, on horseback, intending to arrive at his own home near Independence, seventy miles to the southwest, sometime the following day. When he didn't reach his destination on schedule, family members assumed at first that he had simply tarried longer in Fort Scott than originally planned, but alarm grew with each passing day. On the twenty-fourth, state senator A. M. York set out in search of his missing brother. From Fort Scott, he retraced the doctor's path and spoke with several people who'd seen his brother. About twelve miles west of Parsons in the Drum Creek area of northwest Labette County, the trail turned cold.

Among the places York visited in his futile quest was the wayside inn of a German family named Bender, located along the Osage Trail north of Cherryvale. The family consisted of

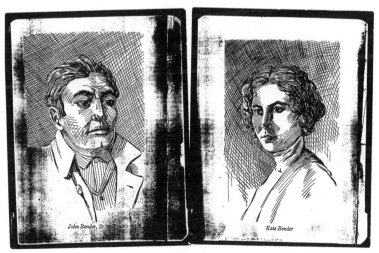

Sketch of Kate and John Bender, from The Benders in Kansas.

sixty-year-old John William Bender, his fifty-five-year-old wife, his twenty-four-year-old stepson John Gebardt (also known as John Bender), and the couple's twenty-two-year-old daughter Kate. The residents told him they had seen no sign of Dr. York in the neighborhood.

At least half a dozen other people had mysteriously disappeared in the same general area during the previous year. Among them was a recent widower named George Lonchor, who had started north from Independence in late November of 1872 with his eighteen-month-old daughter, but his team and wagon were found abandoned at a water hole in the Drum Creek area a few days later. Not until Lonchor's father-in-law traveled to the area around March 1, 1873, and identified the horses and equipment did the disappearance cause a general alarm. Now, coming just a few weeks later, the York disappearance heightened the hysteria and, according to the *Independence South Kansas Tribune,* "created a profound sensation and a public demand that something be done to prevent . . . any more such outrages."

Senator York offered a $100 reward for information leading to the discovery of his brother, dead or alive, and search parties went out day after day in late March and early April scouring the area looking for the missing man. One party called at the Bender residence a second time. John Gebardt led the searchers to a spot about three miles from his home where he claimed he had been shot at the previous Christmas, but the lead proved to be a dead end. It seemed that Dr. York had simply vanished without a trace.

Then, on May 3, a man who happened to be passing the Bender home was attracted by the deserted look of the place. On closer inspection, he discovered no one home and found a starving calf abandoned in a stable. The family had apparently left in a hurry shortly after the second inquiry at their home, and suspicion now rested squarely on the Benders.

The Bender family had settled in the Cherryvale area two years earlier and quickly earned a reputation as an eccentric clan. The old couple spoke very little English and was seldom seen away from their own premises. The stepson, John Gebardt, was considered a "hard case," but young Kate Bender was said to be the ruling spirit of the family. A professed medium, she claimed to have power over evil spirits and to be able to cure all manner of disease, including deafness and blindness. "Professor" Bender had handbills made and distributed throughout the area advertising her clairvoyant services. Kate, who worked briefly as a waitress in a restaurant at a Cherryvale hotel, was usually described as "good looking, well formed," although one reporter claimed she was "a repulsive looking creature." Some folks accused her of witchcraft, and rumors circulated that she and her half-brother lived together as man and wife. No one seemed to know where the family had come from, and now they had disappeared.

When Senator York and others were notified of the deserted Bender home, they hurried to the site and began combing the grounds. Nothing was found until several days later when Senator York, while inspecting a garden behind the house, noticed a depression in the ground similar in shape to a grave. The searchers quickly dug down about

The Bender home on the day bodies were uncovered. (Courtesy Cherryvale Museum)

four feet and unearthed the body of Dr. York. His skull had been bashed from behind, his throat slashed, and his body stripped of clothes except for a shirt.

The next day searchers probed the ground with metal rods and found seven more bodies, including that of Mr. Lonchor and his little girl. All except the child had suffered blows to the head and had their throats cut. The little girl's fully clothed body showed no signs of violence. It was theorized that she had been thrown into the grave with her father while still alive.

Three hammers, thought to be the murder weapons, were found inside the Bender house. The cabin was divided into two rooms by a cloth partition. The front room served as a rest stop for travelers along the Osage Trail, and the room's furniture included a dining table and chairs near the curtain, where meals were served. Under the table, searchers found a trapdoor in the floor, and upon opening it, they discovered a large hole in the ground containing signs of dried blood.

The Benders' ghastly mode of operation seemed clear to investigators. Each victim was coaxed to sit with his back against the curtain so that the outline of his body was visible behind the partition. From the other side of the curtain, the murderer sneaked up behind the unsuspecting traveler with a hammer and dealt him a severe blow to the head. A prompt slit to the throat with a butcher knife finished the deadly work, and the body was dropped into the makeshift cellar until it could be secretly buried. Although only a couple of the victims were thought to be carrying significant amounts of cash or other valuables at the time they were killed, robbery was the only plausible motive officials could cite for the crimes.

As news of the gruesome murders spread, area citizens came forward with tales of bizarre experiences at the Bender inn. A woman recalled paying a visit to Miss Kate Bender during a time of illness. The doctress ministered to the sick woman but declined to take payment for her services unless they proved beneficial. The woman left her sidesaddle with the Benders as a show of good faith and then departed. When the health of the woman failed to improve, she came back one evening to reclaim the saddle and was seated in the front room at the table in the presence of the entire family. According to the *Girard Press*, Kate Bender "invoked the presence of the spirits, and then proceeded to go through a series of incantations, something after the fashion of . . . the breeders of witchcraft in its palmy days." Each member of the family, the report went on the say, "had a large butcher knife which they would draw across their throats and make other significant motions with, and with a uniformity that indicated that they had been thoroughly drilled in this spiritualistic manual of arms."

During a lull in the ceremony, the terror-stricken woman momentarily regained her senses and stepped outside with a show of unconcern, leaving her bonnet behind to suggest she meant to return. Once outside, she fled on foot. The Benders gave chase, but she managed to escape by hiding in tall grass and crawling on her hands and knees.

A man named Charles Hallett told of a time when he stopped at the Bender place. While seated there, he heard a noise behind him and turned around to see a man approaching with a hammer. When Hallett quickly drew his pistol, the man explained with an indignant air that he was simply driving a nail in the floor.

Other people told similar stories, but these after-the-fact recollections were taken with a dash of salt even when they were first put forth. As the editor of the *Girard Press* said, "It seems almost wonderful that these occurrences, mysterious in their nature, have not long ago directed suspicion towards them [the Benders], especially under the excitement existing on account of so many mysterious disappearances."

Outraged citizens flocked to the Bender place, even as bodies were still being dug up, demanding that the villains be hunted down and brought to justice. Posses fanned out looking for any sign of the Benders, telegrams were sent in every direction describing the fugitives, and Kansas governor Thomas A. Osborn issued a proclamation offering a reward of $500 each for their capture. One observer complained that $500 wasn't enough reward for the apprehension of "the most terrible den

GOVERNOR'S PROCLAMATION.

$2,000 REWARD

State of Kansas, Executive Department.

WHEREAS, several atrocious murders have been recently committed in Labette County, Kansas, under circumstances which fasten, beyond doubt, the commissions of these crimes upon a family known as the "Bender family," consisting of

JOHN BENDER, about 60 years of age, five feet eight or nine inches in height, German, speaks but little English, dark complexion, no whiskers, and sparely built;

MRS. BENDER, about 50 years of age, rather heavy set, blue eyes, brown hair, German, speaks broken English;

JOHN BENDER, Jr., alias John Gebardt, five feet eight or nine inches in height, slightly built, gray eyes with brownish tint, brown hair, light moustache, no whiskers, about 27 years of age, speaks English with German accent;

KATE BENDER, about 24 years of age, dark hair and eyes, good looking, well formed, rather bold in appearance, fluent talker, speaks good English with very little German accent:

AND WHEREAS, said persons are at large and fugitives from justice, now therefore, I, Thomas A. Osborn, Governor of the State of Kansas, in pursuance of law, do hereby offer a **REWARD OF FIVE HUNDRED DOLLARS** for the apprehension and delivery to the Sheriff of Labette County, Kansas, of each of the persons above named.

In Testimony Whereof, I have hereunto subscribed my name, and caused the Great Seal of the State to be affixed.

[L. S.]   Done at Topeka, this 17th day of May, 1873.

THOMAS A. OSBORN,
Governor.

By the Governor:

W. H. SMALLWOOD,
Secretary of State.

A replica of the governor's proclamation offering a reward for the apprehension of the Benders. (Courtesy Cherryvale Museum) of murderers and robbers which ever infested the Southwest." In this atmosphere of hysteria, arrest warrants were issued for several area residents suspected of being in league with the Benders, but the accusations later proved groundless. A posse under Deputy U. S. Marshal S. S. Peterson soon picked up the track of a wagon heading away from the Bender place and followed it to Thayer, a small town twelve miles to the north. There the lawmen learned that the Bender wagon and team had been hitched to a rail and abandoned when the family boarded a train for Humboldt, located about twenty-five miles farther north. Telegraphic inquiry, though, revealed that the Benders had disembarked at Chanute, several miles below Humboldt, and bought a ticket for Chetopa, located thirty-five miles southeast of Cherryvale on the southern Kansas border.

The posse hurried back to Labette County, picked up some additional men, including Senator York, and headed for Chetopa on fresh horses. At Oswego, the posse again procured fresh mounts and resumed their swift pursuit. At Chetopa, they learned the Benders had taken a team and wagon southwest into Indian Territory toward the Grand River thirty miles away and that the fugitives had left only about three hours earlier. The posse again took up the chase, hotly pressing the pursuit.

What happened next is not altogether clear even to this day, as contradictory reports filtered back to Kansas towns. One account in late May said that the Benders had been overtaken and "launched into eternity." Another report a few days later said they were still at large and being pursued through Texas and perhaps into Mexico. As one editor stated, "Rumors are so many and contradictory that it is impossible to learn the truth as to the whole situation of the pursuit."

The returning posse confounded inquisitors when not a single one could be prevailed upon to say what had happened. Their conspiracy of silence, however, argues strongly in favor of the report that the Benders had been overtaken and summarily dispatched. It seems likely that the posse's refusal to talk stemmed from a fear they might be held accountable for having taken the law into their own hands.

Later evidence seems to confirm this conclusion. In 1882, for example, a man who'd lived at Independence at the time of the Bender murders gave a statement to a St. Louis newspaper filling in the missing details concerning the chase after the fugitives. He said the posse caught up with the Benders about four miles north of the Grand River, confronted them with the irrefutable evidence of their brutal crimes, and shot all four of them on the spot. The posse then buried the bodies in a common grave.

Still, rumors that the Benders had never been caught persisted. They were reported to be living in Mexico. Another version stated that they had returned to Germany. They were said to be suspects in an Indiana murder case. In 1889, the mystery took another bizarre turn when a McPherson, Kansas, seeress accused two women she had known in Michigan of being Kate Bender and her mother. The two women were brought to Kansas and made to stand trial at the Labette County court in Oswego for the murder of Dr. William York. The women were found not guilty when

Kansas historical marker about the Benders at the intersection of Highways 169 and 400.

the psychic's accusations proved to be the result of a dream. Today the Bender murders are memorialized by a Kansas State Historical Marker at the intersection of Highways 169 and 400 a couple of miles west of the Bender Mounds, where the family lived. Having replaced a similar marker on old Highway 160 (now 400), the new plaque, like its predecessor, stresses the sense of uncertainty surrounding the ultimate fate of the Benders. "Their story," the marker concludes, "is unresolved, and remains one of the great unsolved mysteries of the Old West."

7

The Younger Brothers' Roscoe Gun Battle

By Larry Wood and William Preston Mangum II

Around the second week of March 1874, Pinkerton detectives Louis J. Lull of Chicago and John H. Boyle of St. Louis, checked into the Commercial Hotel, located on the square in Osceola, Missouri, the St. Clair County seat. The pair had been sent into Missouri in response to the Gad's Hill train robbery that had occurred on January 31 in the eastern part of the state. The infamous James-Younger gang was suspected of perpetrating the heist. Lull and Boyle knew the Youngers had relatives in St. Clair County and often hid out there.

Fearing their names might be recognized, Lull and Boyle registered at the hotel as W. J. Allen and James H. Wright, respectively. (Many accounts give "Wright" as the second detective's actual name, but his real name was Boyle and he, like his partner, was using an alias.) To disguise their purpose, the pair spread the word around Osceola that they

The Commercial Hotel in Osceola, where Pinkerton agents stayed, as it appears today.

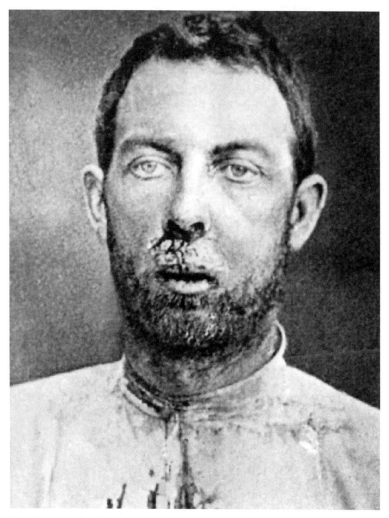

Jim Younger after his capture in Minnesota in 1876. (Courtesy of Legends of America)

were cattle buyers. While in town, they recruited a part-time sheriff's deputy named Edwin B. Daniels to guide them into the countryside where the Youngers' principal haunts were. On March 16, they set out for Roscoe, a village about twelve miles southwest of Osceola. Arriving that evening, they spent the night at the Roscoe House, a local hotel owned by former Quantrill guerrilla Oliver Bunch and his family.

The same night, John Younger, a ladies' man and an avid partygoer, had talked his brother Jim into accompanying him to a dance at the Monegaw Hotel in Monegaw Springs, a small community about five miles northwest of Roscoe. John worked part-time at the hotel, and the Youngers often spent time at the adjacent Log Tavern.

Although Jim was older than John and had ridden briefly with Quantrill near the end of the Civil War, John was considered the wilder and more desperate of the two brothers. In 1866, when he was only fourteen or fifteen, he had killed a man at Independence, Missouri, in what was ruled self-defense, and five years later, he had killed a lawman in Scyene, Texas, a crime for which he was still wanted. His oldest brother, Cole, had recruited him to the James-Younger gang in 1873, and he had recently helped out in the Gad's Hill caper. On the other hand, Jim, by many accounts, had a serious and sensitive nature and had tried to go straight after the war. He had declined to go along to Gad's Hill, and his participation in the escapades of the James-Younger gang had thus far been minimal.

However, he apparently enjoyed himself at the dance in Monegaw Springs, as he and his brother stayed there until late in the evening. After leaving the dance, they spent the night about three miles southeast of Monegaw at the cabin of a black woman named Aunt Hannah McFerrin; her sister had been a longtime servant of the Younger family. In the early afternoon of the next day, they rode to the nearby home of Theodrick Snuffer for lunch. Snuffer was a family friend of long standing with whom the brothers often stayed when they were in the area. He had been a neighbor and a witness to the will of Charles Lee Younger, the Younger brothers' grandfather who had died in St. Clair County in 1854. His son Josiah Snuffer had been a close friend of Cole Younger before Josiah was killed during the Civil War. Cole had also served during the war with another son, Owen Snuffer.

(Owen Snuffer helped *Osceola Democrat* editor Augustus C. Appler pen the first biography of the Younger brothers later in the year of 1874.)

Around the same time that Jim and John Younger left Aunt Hannah's cabin, the three lawmen departed Roscoe and headed north along the old Chalk Level Road. Boyle stopped at the house of a man who lived about a mile outside town and told his partners he would catch up with them later. A mile or two farther on, Lull and Daniels approached Theodrick Snuffer's home. (An alternate version of events says the reason Boyle did not accompany Lull and Daniels to Snuffer's house is that he had served in the Confederate Army with some men from St. Clair County and that he hung back out of sight for fear of being recognized. Being recognized, however, would not have blown his cover unless his former comrades had a way of knowing he wasn't in the cattle business. The simplest explanation for his absence and the one he gave himself is that he had not yet caught up with his partners at the time they approached the Snuffer home.)

Jim and John Younger had just sat down for lunch when they heard the sound of the riders outside the house. They crawled up a ladder into the attic where they could keep an eye on the activity out front by peering through the cracks in the log house. Meanwhile, Snuffer stepped outside to see what the visitors wanted. Explaining that he and his partner were cattle buyers, Lull said they had heard the Widow Sims, who lived nearby, had some animals for sale, and he asked directions to her place.

Snuffer gave the two men the information they requested, but when he came back inside, he remarked to the Youngers, as they descended from the attic, that the men had ridden off in the opposite direction from what he had told them. Instead of going toward the Sims place northeast of Snuffer's farm, they had started in a northwesterly direction on a timber trail that served as a shortcut for travelers along Chalk Level Road and that converged with the main road near Aunt Hannah's cabin.

John had noticed that the younger man (Daniels) had

seemed nervous and that they were both too well armed to be cattle buyers. He wanted to follow the men, but Jim suggested they shouldn't go looking for trouble. While they were still debating the issue, Boyle passed the house and took the same trail his partners had followed earlier. John insisted on investigating, and Jim now agreed to accompany him. The brothers retrieved their horses from the Snuffers' shed, where they had hidden them when they rode in, and they started after the mysterious "cattle buyers." Jim had one of his two pistols drawn, and John had a double-barreled shotgun cradled in his arm as the brothers set out after the detectives along the diagonal trail across a hilly field.

Boyle caught up with Lull and Daniels about half a mile from the Snuffer place, near where the diagonal path merged with Aunt Hannah's road. Aunt Hannah's son-in-law, "Monegaw George" McDonald, lived next door to her, and he was outside in a pasture across the road from his cabin. Fifteen-year-old Ol Davis was also nearby cutting sprouts along the fencerow of his father's farm. After the lawmen reunited, they started down the road with Boyle taking the lead and Lull and Daniels riding along in the rear at a walk.

Suddenly, Jim and John Younger came charging up the diagonal trail onto the main road and ordered them to halt. Boyle bolted through a field at first sight of them. Jim yelled for him to stop, but he kept riding as fast as he could. Jim fired his pistol at the fleeing lawman, knocking his hat off his head but doing no other damage.

The Youngers told the other two men, who had obeyed the order to halt, to drop their weapons, and they complied. Jim dismounted and picked up the revolvers, one of which was an expensive, English-made, .45-caliber Tranter. Remarking that they were "damn fine pistols," he mockingly thanked Lull for making a "present" of them. The Youngers asked where the men were from, and Lull replied that they were cattle buyers from Osceola.

"What are you doing out here?" one of the brothers demanded.

"Just rambling around," Lull replied.

Unconvinced, John said he knew Lull had been in these parts before, and he demanded to know if the two men were detectives. Lull at first denied that he had been in the area previously, but when John said he had seen him at Monegaw Springs, the lawman admitted he had been there a few days earlier. He still denied, however, that he was a detective or that he had been looking for the Youngers. Deputy Sheriff Daniels tried to explain that he wasn't a detective and offered to show proof of who he was and where he was from, but one of the brothers remarked that he already knew him. John then asked why the pair had so many weapons if they weren't detectives. Lull responded that it wasn't safe to travel without arms and that they had as much right to carry guns as anyone else. John retorted that he didn't need any smart-aleck remarks, and he leveled his shotgun at the two men in a threatening manner.

While Jim was still busy confiscating the pistols, Daniels made a comment that briefly drew John's attention, and Lull seized the opportunity. Although he may not have known the precise identity of the men he faced, Lull surely knew they were part of the James-Younger gang, and he knew the danger he and his partner were in. Just a week earlier, on March 10, fellow Pinkerton agent Joseph Whicher had been killed in Clay County, reportedly by Frank James and others, when he had gone there to try to track down the James brothers. Lull must have sensed that he and Daniels now faced a similar fate.

Reaching beneath his coat, he quickly pulled out a small No. 2 Smith & Wesson pistol, cocked it, and fired a shot that struck John in the neck. Some reports suggest that he also may have fired a second shot that gave Jim a flesh wound. Spooked by the gunfire, Lull's horse reared uncontrollably. As it turned to run, John managed to fire his shotgun even though he was gravely wounded, and the blast struck the detective in the arm and shoulder. While Lull fought to control his horse, Jim, still standing in the road, knocked Daniels out of the saddle with a shot to the neck, killing him almost instantly.

An old historic monument along Chalk Level Road marking the spot where Detective Lull fell.

Lull took off down the road, but, because of his wounded arm, he continued to have trouble controlling his horse. With his rage keeping him in the saddle, John drew a pistol and started after Lull. Just a hundred feet or so down the road, the detective's intractable horse plunged through some brush and trees, causing it to slow down. John rode up beside

A new historic marker about the Younger-Pinkerton gunfight at the intersection of Chalk Level Road and present-day Highway E, just west of the old marker.

Lull and fired two shots. One missed, but the other struck the detective squarely in the left side of his chest. Sinking in the saddle from his wounds, Lull now lost all control of his horse and was knocked to the ground by a low-hanging limb.

Barely clinging to life, John turned and started back toward his brother. Jim, who had been checking on Daniels to see if he was dead, looked up to see John reeling in the saddle with blood pouring from his wound as he approached. He called his brother's name as John fell from his horse into a pigpen on the other side of a fence.

George McDonald, or "Speed" as he was usually called, had glanced up from his chores at the sound of gunfire and hurried to the edge of the road to see what was going on. He was standing near the place where John Younger had fallen as Jim rushed up to his dying brother. Receiving no response when he tried to talk to John, Jim removed his brother's pistols, watch, and other personal items and tossed one of the pistols to McDonald for safekeeping. He told Speed to catch one of the horses and ride over to tell Theodrick Snuffer what had happened. Jim then mounted John's horse and raced away in pursuit of Boyle.

Chalk Level Road, where the Younger-Pinkerton gunfight took place, as it appears today.

Having feigned death until after Jim was gone, Lull, despite his serious wounds, rose and staggered across the road before falling again.

Ol Davis's father, John, soon arrived on the scene and found Daniels lying face down in the muddy trail. Turning the body over, he saw blood running from the deputy's nose and mouth, and he could tell Daniels was dead. After examining the body of John Younger and deciding that he, too, was dead, Davis found Lull propped against a tree, near where he had collapsed after crossing the road. Lull said he hoped he had fallen into good hands, and Davis assured the detective that he wasn't there to harm him. Apparently, not all the locals were in a benevolent mood. While Lull lay beside the road, an unidentified bystander reportedly walked up and suggested that someone should "finish" the detective.

On his way to the Snuffer home, Speed McDonald met Theodrick Snuffer, who had been attracted by the sound of gunfire, starting up the road, and told him what had happened. Another version of events says Speed, rather than mounting a horse himself, sent a messenger to deliver the news of what had happened and then went back to stand guard over John's body to keep the hogs from bothering it.

Quickly realizing his pursuit of Boyle was futile, Jim returned to the vicinity of the shootout, where, according to one report, he helped move his brother inside Aunt Hannah's cabin. (This however, conflicts with the testimony of John McFerrin, Aunt Hannah's husband, who said the last he saw of Jim Younger was when Jim came down the road on foot to check on his brother.) Although most accounts say John was already dead when brought into the home, having died where he fell, another version alleges he was unconscious but still clinging to life when brought inside and died very soon afterwards. A contemporaneous newspaper account that reported John Younger lived five or ten minutes after he fell seems to support the latter version.

After tending to his brother, Jim rode to tell Theodrick Snuffer the details of what had happened and to make arrangements for Snuffer to take care of John's body. Jim then fled the scene altogether and later that evening was supposedly spotted north of Monegaw Springs bleeding profusely from wounds he had received in the gunfight. The report, if true, was certainly exaggerated, because what is known for sure is that Jim started for Arkansas the same evening to find his brothers, Cole and Bob, and give them the bad news.

After Jim Younger left, Lull was taken to the front porch of Aunt Hannah's cabin, where his wounds were seared. Then the wounded detective was taken inside, and Daniels's body was moved to the porch.

When news of the shooting reached Roscoe that evening, a party of citizens from the community, including a young man named David Crowder, went to the scene of the encounter to tend to the wounded and dead men. Crowder, John Davis's future son-in-law, spent the night in the room where John Younger's body lay, guarding it with a shotgun to make sure enemies of the Youngers did not try to steal or mutilate it. According to legend, a young woman with a pistol strapped to her waist, thought to be John Younger's sister Henrietta, appeared in the room sometime after dark and paced the floor most of the night without speaking a word to Crowder.

On the morning of March 18, a coroner's jury was conducted over the dead bodies of John Younger and Ed Daniels at the McFerrin cabin with Justice of the Peace James St. Clair of Roscoe presiding. Lull was the principal witness in the case. Still maintaining his alias, he offered a fairly detailed account of the affray that had left him gravely wounded. Others testifying before the jury included Speed McDonald, Theodrick Snuffer, Aunt Hannah's husband John, her son John, and Drs. A. C. Marquis and L. Lewis, who examined the dead men. The six-man jury, with Roscoe merchant Alonza Ray serving as foreman, determined "that John Younger came to his death by a pistol shot, supposed to be in the hands of W. J. Allen," and "that Edward B. Daniels came to his death by a pistol shot, supposed to have been fired by the hand of James Younger."

Afterwards, John Younger was buried in a shallow grave beneath a large cedar tree on the Snuffer farm, and Lull was taken by spring wagon to Roscoe. (Most accounts say Lull was taken to Roscoe on the evening of the shootout, but the contemporaneous evidence does not seem to support this.) Upon his arrival at Roscoe, Detective Lull was placed in a second-floor room of the Roscoe House.

The same morning, Boyle finally reached Osceola and reported to Sheriff James Johnson that his fellow detectives had been captured and that he had heard shooting as he rode away. Friends of Daniels immediately set out for the McFerrin neighborhood to ascertain the situation. After going part way, they met a rider who told them Daniels and John Younger were dead and that Lull was seriously wounded. They returned to Osceola with the news, throwing the town into a frenzy of excitement.

A hack was sent out for the body of Daniels, and Johnson dispatched a posse under Deputy Simpson Beckley to the Roscoe area to learn the details of what had taken place

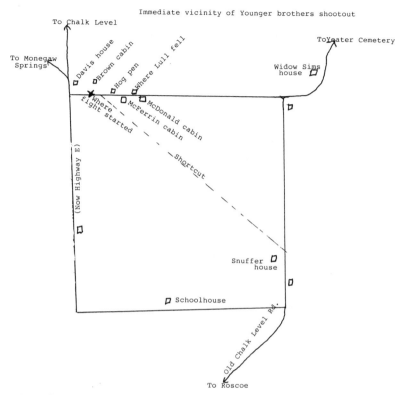

Sketch/map of area where the Younger-Pinkerton gunfight occurred.

and to prevent further violence. Detective Boyle supposedly declined to join the posse and, by some accounts, fled Osceola and was never heard from again.

On the evening of the eighteenth, Theodrick Snuffer, Speed McDonald, and David Crowder reinterred the body of John Younger in the Yeater Cemetery northeast of the Snuffer farm (not southeast as many accounts say). John's friend and half-uncle, T. J. Younger, a county judge, was summoned from Appleton City about sixteen miles away to attend the service, but it's not clear whether he made the trip. John's body was buried at an angle from northwest to southeast, supposedly so that it would face Dixie. A more mundane explanation is that, unwilling to mark the site with a stone for fear that

John's body would be disturbed, his friends laid him to rest in a diagonal grave for easy identification by family and loved ones. Despite the precaution of not marking the grave, John's friends, including Aunt Hannah and the Widow Sims, took turns standing guard with a shotgun for several days following the burial to make sure the body was not disturbed.

Around the same time John Younger was buried, the body of Ed Daniels arrived in Osceola, where it was claimed by his sister and her husband, a local banker. The body was buried in the Osceola Cemetery on March 20, and the grave was marked with a large, white marble slab.

Drs. Marquis and Lewis thought at first that Lull's wounds would not be fatal, but the detective soon took a turn for the worse. His wife, Marian, was summoned from Chicago on March 19, and she arrived shortly afterwards, along with William Pinkerton of the Pinkerton Detective Agency. Dr. D. C. McNeil, whose sixteen-year-old daughter Cora was Jim Younger's girlfriend, was called in to attend the sinking patient. As Lull lay on his death bed, his partner John Boyle, who had supposedly fled the territory, also turned up. Lull died on March 21, and his body was taken by wagon to nearby Clinton. From there, it was shipped by rail to Chicago and buried in Rose Hill Cemetery. A popular legend, however, claims Lull did not die but rather faked his own death to avoid the vengeance of the Younger gang.

After rendezvousing with Cole and Bob in Arkansas, Jim Younger went his separate way for awhile but reunited with his brothers and other members of the James-Younger gang in September of 1876 for the ill-fated Northfield, Minnesota, bank robbery. All three Younger brothers were captured shortly after the fiasco and sentenced to life in prison. Bob died while still in prison, and Jim and Cole were paroled in 1901 after serving almost twenty-five years. Jim longed for a complete pardon, which would allow him to return to Missouri and try to live a normal life. Always introspective, he grew increasingly reclusive and despondent as he watched his hopes dim. On October 19, 1902, Jim Younger killed himself in a hotel room at St. Paul, Minnesota. His body was brought back to Lee's Summit in Jackson County, Missouri, for burial, about seventy miles from where his brother John had been buried twenty-eight years earlier.

After 130 years, traces of the fateful events that took place along Chalk Level Road on that cold day of March 17, 1874, are still apparent. In 1934, the Community Women's Association, an organization headed by Ms. Augusta Shram, who had been acquainted with the Younger brothers, erected a monument commemorating the Pinkerton-Youngers shootout. Marking the spot where Detective Lull fell, the monument was placed at the side of the road across from where Aunt Hannah's cabin stood.

In 1989, a new monument in the form of a large stone map was placed near where the fight began, a couple of hundred feet west of the old marker at the corner of Aunt Hannah's road and present-day Highway E.

Sometime after John Younger's burial in Yeater Cemetery, a bent, metal bar was stuck in the ground to mark the grave. Over the years, the bar grew rusty and the burial site more and more forlorn. Finally in the mid 1990s a proper stone was placed at the head of John Younger's diagonal grave. Although slightly modernized, the old Commercial Hotel, where the Pinkertons stayed from early to mid March of 1874 and where the Youngers had stayed on previous occasions, still stands on the square in Osceola. And at times, when the wind blows off Little Monegaw Creek, the ghosts of the notorious Younger brothers are said to be heard at the base of Mount Monegaw, near where the old Log Tavern stood. It seems they never left.

8

Hobbs Kerry and the Otterville Train Robbery

Within weeks after the James-Younger gang's holdup of the train near Otterville in Cooper County, Missouri, on July 7, 1876, twenty-three-year-old Hobbs Kerry was arrested in southwest Missouri for his role in the crime. He was taken back to the central part of the state, and he soon implicated the other members of the gang. Many authors have portrayed Kerry as a raw recruit whose youth and inexperience led to his quick capture and eager confession, but Kerry's background suggests that he was more reckless than naïve.

The son of an English-born schoolteacher, Kerry moved with his family from Arkansas to the rowdy mining camp of Granby, Missouri, in the late 1850s when he was a small child. He and his older brothers, Albert and Toby, grew up among the rough characters frequenting the booming camp and became miners themselves during their youth. (Previous authors have spelled Kerry's name with a "K," and that spelling has been accepted for the purposes of this chapter. However, there is considerable evidence to suggest the actual spelling was "Carey.")

During the summer of 1870, according to a local newspaper, Granby was "favored with a small installment of 'civilization' in the shape of a bevy of Cyprians" who camped on the outskirts of town, where the boys and men of the rip-roaring mining town congregated to pass their time. On July 17, Toby Kerry was among the young men gathered at the "Cyprian camp" when he and an Arkansas man named Bennett got into a row over a card game. Both men pulled out their pistols and fired twice without effect, but Bennett got off a third shot that killed Kerry instantly. Some of Kerry's friends rushed to his defense, but Bennett took temporary shelter in a nearby cornfield until his companions helped him mount his horse and "started him for the 'tall timber.'" Toby Kerry was buried at Granby the next day.

The Kerry brothers evidently had a predilection for sporting women, because a year later, Albert Kerry killed a man in Granby in a dispute that also involved a prostitute. According to the nearby *Neosho Times,* "a slippery cyprian named Mollie Howard" was the cause of the difficulty that led Kerry to shoot J. S. Dunlap on July 4, 1871.

Apparently, no charges were filed, and in October of 1873, when Granby was fully organized as a town, Albert Kerry was made city marshal. His new role as primary peacekeeper in the community, though, was not enough to deflect suspicion two months later when a man named John Cole was found shot to death outside a Granby saloon. Albert Kerry, his brother Hobbs, and a third man were arrested and charged with the December 6 murder, but they were released shortly afterwards for lack of evidence.

Shortly after this incident, Hobbs Kerry left Granby for the mining fields of Colorado, but he was back within a couple of months, declaring that the prospects for mining were better at Granby than anywhere else and that he wouldn't leave again. In May of 1874, he began building a home in Granby as a demonstration of that promise.

However, by late 1875, he had had a change of heart, and he moved to the livelier mining town of Joplin twenty miles away. There he met Bruce Younger, half-uncle to Cole Younger and his brothers. He also got to know Sam Wells (alias Charlie Pitts), whose father had been a neighbor of the Younger family in Lee's Summit, Missouri, and Bill Stiles (alias Bill Chadwell). Bruce said Cole and Bob Younger had recently visited him in Joplin, and Kerry and his three new friends began kicking around the idea of recruiting Bruce's infamous kinfolk to help them hold up the bank in Granby.

After spending the winter in Joplin, the four men crossed the state line into Kansas in the late spring of 1876 and took jobs in the coal mines near Scammon. Tiring of the hard work,

Bruce Younger soon left his companions and pulled out of the scheme to hold up the Granby bank. Meanwhile, Chadwell made a trip to central Missouri to recruit the Younger brothers for the job, and he reported that they were coming down.

When they had not arrived a week later, though, Kerry, Pitts, and Chadwell grew impatient and started north in late June to link up with the famous outlaws. Failing to locate the Youngers at their stomping grounds around Monegaw Springs, the three men rode on to Jackson County, where they ran into Frank James. He directed them to Dick Tyler's house in another part of the county. There they met Cole Younger, Jesse James, Bob Younger, and Clell Miller.

The outlaws divided into two groups and rode east, reuniting at California, Missouri, on July 4. Two days later, they started back west in pairs and once again reunited on July 7 about two miles east of the bridge where the Missouri Pacific Railroad crossed the Lamine River east of Otterville. Near sundown, six members of the gang went down to the bridge and took the watchman captive while, according to Kerry, he and Chadwell stayed behind at the rendezvous point. Then at 10:30 that night, at a spot near the rendezvous point called Rocky Cut, the same six outlaws forced the watchman to flag down a train bound from Kansas City to St. Louis, while Kerry and Chadwell once again acted mainly as lookouts. Just to be sure, the outlaws had placed ties on the track to stop the train, and when it came to a halt, they started firing their pistols, quickly boarded the train, and took an estimated $15,000 from the express safes.

After the robbery, the gang rode south throughout the night and stopped on the morning of July 8 seventeen miles southeast of Sedalia and divided the loot. Kerry's share was about $1,200. Afterwards, the gang split up, with Pitts, Chadwell, and Kerry riding together. On the morning of July 9, Kerry left his two partners and took a train from Montrose to Fort Scott, Kansas. That evening he went on to Parsons, and the next morning he took a train to Granby by way of Vinita in Indian Territory. During the next three weeks,

Kerry divided his time between Granby and Joplin, where he reunited with Bruce Younger, and he also managed a brief trip to Indian Territory to see his brother, Albert.

Back in June before the plot to rob the Granby bank fell through, St. Louis detectives had gotten wind of the scheme and made a trip to the area to investigate. Suspecting that

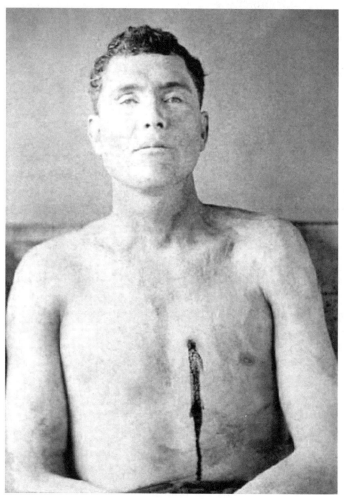

Kerry's sidekick Bill Caldwell was killed at Northfield, Minnesota, two months after the Otterville caper. (Courtesy Legends of America)

some of the same men who had planned the Granby job were involved in the train robbery, the lawmen returned to southwest Missouri after the Otterville caper. Upon learning that Kerry had also returned after a period of absence and had been flashing money around, they arrested him in Granby on July 31 on suspicion and took him back to St. Louis. (A week later Bruce Younger was also arrested but soon released.)

Kerry, who had only twenty dollars on him when arrested, was transferred to Sedalia, where he gave a statement on August 4 implicating the other seven members of the outlaw gang. He was then sent to Boonville to await trial.

Meanwhile, a plot was already afoot among the remaining gang members to make what Cole Younger called one last haul. Shortly after Kerry's confession, a letter appeared in the *Kansas City Times*, purportedly from Jesse James, denouncing Kerry as a "notorious liar and poltroon." But Kerry's statement was generally accepted and may have prompted the gang to hasten their plans. By late August, the same seven men who had robbed the Otterville train, plus Jim Younger to replace the jailed Kerry, were heading north toward Minnesota and a date with destiny. On September 7, 1876, Bill Chadwell and Clell Miller were killed during the ill-fated Northfield Bank robbery, and two weeks later, Charlie Pitts was killed and the Younger brothers captured by a posse sent out in pursuit. Only the James brothers escaped to carry on their outlaw careers.

In part, no doubt, because of his cooperation with authorities, Kerry was let off with a light sentence of four years in prison for obstructing a railroad. When he was admitted to the Missouri State Penitentiary at Jefferson City on April 18, 1877, he was described as 5'8½" in height with light hair, brown eyes, a fair complexion, and large, sharp nose. A comment in the remarks section of the admission register noted that the new prisoner needed to write his mother at Granby. Kerry was released on April 7, 1880, under the three-quarters law, but what happened to him afterwards has not been determined.

9

Red Hot Rivals

When prospectors struck a pocket of rich lead ore on Cherokee County's Short Creek in southeast Kansas during the spring of 1877, miners, entrepreneurs, and assorted adventurers of every stripe rushed to the area in search of quick riches. On Sunday, April 15, just two weeks after the discovery, a party from Columbus, Kansas, went down to the "diggings" and reported "over fifteen hundred miners already on the ground and others coming in by the scores."

A week later, the editors of the *Columbus Republican Courier* paid a visit to the mining camp and "found a wilderness full of men and a city springing up where but two weeks ago there was naught but barren hills and scrubby timber." A town called Empire City was being started on the north side of Short Creek, and houses, stores, and other buildings were going up at the rate of about twelve a day. Five saloons were up and running, and the editors remarked wryly that many of the men seemed to be doing their "prospecting" at these establishments.

During the first week of May, the "Discovery" shaft yielded 50,000 pounds of lead ore, which was selling for thirty-four dollars per thousand. Seven other shafts also were making "big money," and several more were paying expenses. Another town, named Galena, was being laid out on the south side of Short Creek.

By the middle of May, more than eleven hundred shafts had been opened. Prospectors had erected 135 buildings, and hundreds of other new arrivals were camping out in tents, dugouts, and wagons. In all, thirty-five hundred people were living on Short Creek.

On May 15, 1877, the Galena Town Company was organized and immediately began selling lots south of Short Creek. They sold "like hot cakes" for seventy-five dollars and up. By early June all the lots in the original town site had been sold, and many also had been purchased in a new addition called East Galena.

Early-day Galena, Kansas (Courtesy Galena Mining Museum)

North of Short Creek, the Empire Town Company located its town on top of the hills overlooking the stream about a half-mile removed from the creek. The town site was surveyed on May 21, 1877, and two days later, a formal ceremony to dedicate the new town was held. Immediately afterward, the company set up a pine table beneath an oak tree and sold about one hundred lots on the spot to the gathered crowd. By early June, 225 had been sold, and many buildings that had been thrown up pell-mell along the creek during the stampede to the area earlier in the spring were removed from the "old town" to the new town site.

The frenzy of activity in the mining fields surrounding Galena and Empire was matched by the bustle and carousing in the streets of the fledgling towns. Center of the revelry was Bottom Street, an east-west street at the extreme north edge of Galena in the Short Creek valley. Usually called "Red Hot" Street, it was two blocks long and formed the connecting link between the two towns. According to one observer, Red Hot Street richly deserved its fiery sobriquet because of its abundance of "saloons, gambling places, low dance houses, and houses of repute."

Incidents such as the one that occurred Saturday night, June 16, 1877, enhanced Red Hot Street's notoriety. William "Tiger Bill" St. Clair and Harry Campbell were eating supper in Dykeman's Restaurant when four men, avenging an old grudge, came in and promptly opened fire on them, mortally wounding Tiger Bill and slightly wounding Campbell. Several local men pursued the gunmen and briefly exchanged fire with them south of Red Hot Street before the assailants made their escape. (Bob Layton, later identified as one of the gunmen, was himself killed in the fall of 1879 at Batesville, Arkansas.)

Almost from the very beginning of the Short Creek boom, an intense rivalry developed between Empire City and Galena, as each town claimed to be the more prosperous. Rival editors of the *Galena Miner* and the *Empire City Mining Echo* sniped at each other over which town was more prosperous and which was producing more lead. In addition, each side accused the other of using unfair inducements to attract new residents. By early June, outside observers already were commenting on "this little strife between the two towns."

Empire was incorporated as a third-class city on June 18, and

Short Creek as it appears today.

Galena was incorporated as a third-class city the following day. Both elected city officers on June 30. Empire City, however, went Galena one better on July 28 when Gov. George Anthony proclaimed Empire a city of the second class.

Throughout the late spring and early summer, Empire City, backed by its influential leaders, more than held its own with Galena in population, buildings erected, and ore turned in. However, the lack of a clear border between the rival towns and the unfavorable location of Empire City served to blunt any advantage it might otherwise have enjoyed.

The actual dividing line between the two towns was several hundred feet south of Short Creek, and most of the mines along the creek, even many of those on the south side, belonged to the Empire Mining Company (affiliated with the Empire Town Company). Nonetheless, the creek appeared to casual observers as a natural boundary, and many people automatically associated any activity on the south side of the creek with Galena. So, Galena sometimes was credited with assets that rightly belonged to its rival.

More disturbing to Empire City leaders was the fact that the miners tended to do business and seek entertainment in Galena because it was nearer the creek. Empire City apparently had made a mistake in locating its town site on the summit of the hills a half-mile north of the stream.

Empire City sought a way to rectify the situation. In late June, someone suggested erecting a barrier as a line of demarcation between the two towns. When Galena residents first learned of the proposal, they laughed it off as a silly notion. But in late July when Empire City passed a resolution authorizing the rumored stockade and workers actually started setting eight-foot timbers upright in the ground close enough to make a continuous wall between the two towns, the laughter turned to scorn. The *Galena Miner* decried the fence as a blatant attempt to prevent miners from patronizing Galena businesses and to keep Empire City businesses from relocating in Galena. Empire City, the editors asserted, was even trying to shut Galena off from its main source of drinking water, a spring that happened to be on Empire land. The *Empire City Mining Echo* countered that the stockade was being built primarily as a "sanitary precaution" to retard the "filthy stench" emanating from Red Hot Street and as a screen to block from view "this vile locality" and "the lewd practices" of its "fallen creatures."

The stockade was completed around August 1, except for a one-hundred-foot gap across Red Hot Street's west end, which was left open to allow for passing traffic. In the wee hours of the morning of August 22, a party from Empire City went to work closing even this remaining opening. Soon a mob of protesters from Galena gathered and started hurling insults as well as more substantial objects. One worker was shot and slightly wounded in the melee, and the rest of the workers quickly retired. G. W. Webb, mayor of Galena, appeared on the scene, hastily scribbled a proclamation declaring the stockade a nuisance, and read it to the crowd. The work of destroying the stockade then began in earnest. By daylight, the entire fence, nearly a mile long, had been torn down and the timbers set ablaze.

Empire made a demonstration of rebuilding the stockade

Looking toward Short Creek and Empire City from the north edge of present-day Galena.

in the early fall but work stopped, and the incomplete fence came down when a circuit judge at Columbus declared it illegal. About the same time, the shanties along Red Hot Street also were removed so the land could be mined. By late autumn, the falling price of lead had slowed the production of ore, and animosity between the two towns gradually abated with the fading mining fever and cooling weather. The following spring a temperance movement took hold in the Short Creek communities, and a clampdown on "disorderly houses" soon followed. Empire and Galena gradually evolved from rip-roaring mining camps into peaceful towns with all the trappings of respectability.

Lead and zinc mining on Short Creek continued well into the twentieth century, and Galena increasingly became the hub of activity in the area. Empire City was finally annexed into Galena in 1907. Today, it sits like a ghostly prominence on the hills north of the creek, its homes and few remaining abandoned store buildings surrounded by barren mining fields. The water flow in Short Creek has slowed to a mere trickle, and the saloons and "amusement bazaars" in the bottom are long gone. Even today, though, you can walk into the local historical society on Galena's West Seventh Street and find someone eager to swap stories about the "red hot" days and the "stockade wars" of 1877.

10

The Day George Shepherd
"Killed" Jesse James

Around ten o'clock on Sunday morning, November 2, 1879, a Joplin, Missouri, physician named Dr. Burns was driving his buggy in the vicinity of Shoal Creek five miles southwest of the city on his way to a house call. Suddenly shots rang out in the distance up ahead. A few moments later, a one-eyed horseman, brandishing a pistol in each hand, came charging down the road toward the startled doctor. "I've just shot a man back there!" shouted the rider, later identified as George Shepherd, as he galloped past. Dr. Burns saw blood gushing from a bullet wound in the man's leg.

Dr. Burns noticed the approach of two more riders, who seemed to be following Shepherd's trail. They accosted the doctor and told him there was an injured man back there who needed his attention. They added that they had seen a dead man being carried off from the same area. Burns followed the two riders as requested and found a man, whom he later learned was Jim Cummins, suffering from a serious gunshot wound to the side, but no dead body. Burns treated the man's wound and then, satisfied that his patient would recover, wended his way back to Joplin. There he told an altered version of his story that omitted the fact he had treated one of the shooting victims, presumably because he didn't want to involve himself in what appeared to be foul play.

Meanwhile, George Shepherd made his way to Galena, Kansas, a fledgling mining village on Short Creek five miles to the north. According to the town newspaper, "the throng on the streets of Galena was thrown into the wildest excitement and confusion," as Shepherd started proclaiming to anyone who would listen that he had just killed the notorious outlaw Jesse James. He "offered a bleeding and mangled leg in corroboration of his story" and was soon checked into a local hotel to have the injury attended to.

Shepherd, a former Quantrill bushwhacker, had led a group of guerrillas, including young Jesse James, to Texas at the tail end of the war, but then in 1866, Jesse had teamed up with Bloody Bill Anderson's brother Jim to kill Shepherd's nephew Ike Flannery near Rocheport, Missouri. Shepherd had reportedly avenged the murder a year later by killing Jim Anderson on the grounds of the courthouse at Sherman, Texas. Despite the feud, Shepherd joined the James gang and took part in the 1868 Russellville, Kentucky, bank robbery, one of the first robberies attributed to the gang. Shepherd spent a short term in the Kentucky penitentiary for his role in the robbery. Upon his release, he returned home to Jackson County, Missouri, and went straight.

When lead was discovered in southeast Kansas in the late 1870s, he had gone to Short Creek to work in the mines, but at the time the James gang robbed the Glendale train in Jackson County in October of 1879, he was back home working as a teamster. Kansas City marshal James Liggett enlisted Shepherd to infiltrate the gang and help capture the robbers by keeping the marshal apprised of the gang's movements. In return for his cooperation, Shepherd figured to pick up a handsome reward. This much Liggett confirmed; however, only Shepherd himself could attest to many of the other details of his story, particularly the sensational claim that he had killed Jesse James.

According to Shepherd, he went to the home of Jesse's mother, Zerelda Samuel, near Kearney, Missouri, from where he was led blindfolded to the gang's nearby hideout. When the blindfold was removed, he stood facing Jesse James; Jim Cummins, another former Quantrill guerrilla; Ed Miller, whose brother had been killed in the Younger-James gang's botched Northfield, Minnesota, bank robbery; Sam Kaufman; and a man named Taylor. During the ensuing conversation, Jesse stated that his brother Frank had died of consumption a few months earlier.

Shepherd succeeded in gaining the men's confidence, and the gang soon headed for Texas. On the way, they decided to

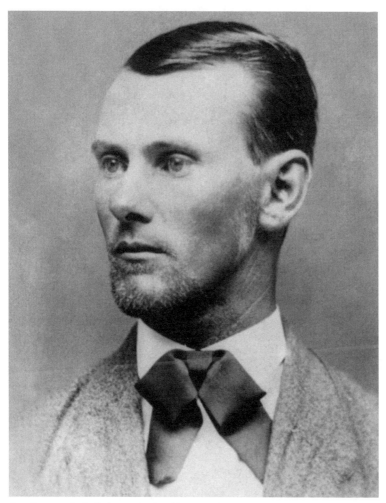

Jesse James as he looked near the time Shepherd claimed to have killed him. (Courtesy Legends of America)

rob a bank at Empire, Galena's rival mining community on the opposite bank of Short Creek. Shepherd hatched a plan with Liggett's deputies to capture the gang during the holdup. However, on his final reconnaissance of the bank, Jesse spotted a guard who'd been stationed there by the marshal. Jesse called off the escapade, and he and the gang proceeded south. Shepherd, however, lingered in town concocting another impromptu scheme, this time with some old mining buddies. Shepherd determined to kill Jesse, then lead the rest of the gang into an ambush set up by his accomplices.

When Shepherd caught up with the gang a mile or two outside Galena, Jesse expressed suspicion at the length of Shepherd's stay in town, but the march resumed, and Shepherd fell in beside Jesse awaiting an opportunity to put his desperate design into action. After the group had ridden a short distance, Jesse turned to one side, and Shepherd promptly pulled his revolver. "This is for killing Ike Flannery!" he announced as he shot the robber chief through the head at close range.

When Shepherd bolted away, Cummins and Kaufman gave chase while Miller tended to Jesse. Cummins outdistanced his partner and soon engaged Shepherd in a running

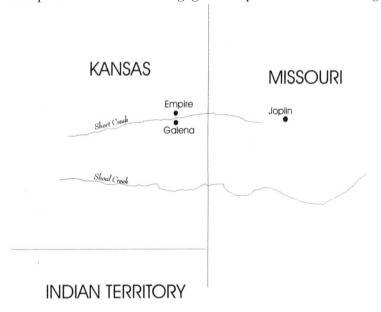

Shooting incident occurred south of Galena near the intersection of Shoal Creek and the state line.

Map showing the area where the shooting incident occurred.

gun battle. Shepherd hoped to lead his pursuers into the prearranged ambush, but his confederates either were farther away than he expected or failed to show altogether. Seeing that Cummins was about to overtake him, Shepherd wheeled his horse and faced the oncoming rider in a brief showdown that left both men wounded. When Kaufman saw his injured partner retiring from the fray, he called off his dilatory pursuit. He and Cummins started back to join their fallen leader as Shepherd galloped away.

Shepherd's tale was greeted almost immediately with doubt. Moreover, suspicion grew when a party of citizens from Galena traveled to the scene of the skirmish on Sunday afternoon to look for Jesse's body and came back shortly after dark "without any intelligence." Lawmen from Joplin crossed the state line to aid in the investigation, and the next day, Monday, November 3, Marshall Liggett arrived from Kansas City to lead a posse in a fruitless search for the outlaws.

As a bold headline in the *Galena Miner* playfully stated a week later, the question that faced an excited public was "Whether Jesse James, the Robber Chief Lies Dead, or George Shepherd Lies Living." The consensus around the Joplin-Galena area favored the latter conclusion. Jasper County deputy sheriff Payton, who'd gone to Short Creek on Sunday evening, told a *Joplin Herald* reporter the next day that "I saw Shepherd, and he said he was positive he had killed Jesse James, but for all that I do not believe he did." Dr. Burns seemed to be among the few men who accepted Shepherd's story. He felt convinced, based presumably on what he had been told by the two men who had solicited his help, that a killing had taken place.

The Shepherd affair caused a stir not just locally, but throughout the region. When word reached the Kansas City area, Jesse's mother joined the chorus of those who discredited Shepherd's account of events. She scoffed at the notion that a "one-eyed man," who was "slow as an ox" to boot, could get the drop on her Jesse. She claimed that Shepherd had not come to her home in October as he had stated and that, in fact, she hadn't seen him in years. There were those who pointed out, however, that Mrs. Samuel might naturally want to deny that she had had anything to do with arranging a meeting that had indirectly led to her son's death. Speculation about whether Jesse was alive or dead continued for several weeks. The whole state of Missouri buzzed with rumors. In mid November, Jesse James was reported alive and well in Texas. Late in the month, he and his gang were said to still be in the area of Short Creek. About the same time, a Kansas City newspaper reported that Jim Cummins had returned to northern Missouri and confirmed Shepherd's story. On December 2, the *Joplin Herald* said that Jesse James was presumed dead. A report from Richmond, Missouri, three days later claimed that a wagon carrying the remains of Jesse's decomposing body had been spotted heading for the James home in Clay County. Then a doctor was said to have visited Marshall Liggett and told him that he had issued a death certificate before turning Jesse's body over to friends. A later account said the coffin bearing the infamous outlaw's corpse had arrived at Kearney by train and that Jesse James was now lying "beneath Clay County turf."

Much conjecture also centered on George Shepherd's motives. If his story was true, why had he killed Jesse James? No doubt, he hoped to collect a reward, and Shepherd himself added that he was also acting to avenge Ike Flannery's death. Cole Younger and others pointed to the Russellville bank robbery as the cause of the rift between Shepherd and Jesse James. Cole said that, after Shepherd's release from the Kentucky penitentiary, Jesse feared Shepherd might implicate him in the crime. Shepherd's brother Mac said that George blamed Jesse for his imprisonment. When George was first jailed in Kentucky, members of the gang tried to raise bond money to go toward his bail, but Jesse supposedly refused to contribute and, therefore, the gang failed to raise the requisite amount. Another observer suggested that George somehow blamed Jesse for the death of his cousin Oliver Shepherd, who was killed by deputies sent out to arrest him after the Russellville robbery. Cole Younger also added that there had been, at one time, a dispute between George Shepherd and Jesse James over a woman.

Opinions varied, too, among those who felt Shepherd was lying. Many suggested that Jesse and his gang, not Shepherd, had instigated the skirmish south of Galena because they suspected Shepherd of betraying the gang to authorities. Others speculated that Jesse James, acting in cahoots with Shepherd, had staged the shootout in order to share in his own reward money and to give himself the added advantage of being thought dead. This, however, seems unlikely, given the severity of Shepherd's and Jim Cummins's wounds.

George Shepherd was disturbed by all the bad publicity he received for "killing" Jesse James. He claimed to have received more criticism for this one act than Jesse and his gang ever did for all of their misdeeds. In response to Shepherd's lament, John N. Edwards, Quantrill's first biographer and the James brothers' chief apologist, pointed out that no one liked a traitor.

Although speculation swirled for weeks following George Shepherd's dramatic announcement on the streets of Galena, few sober minds continued to believe for very long that Jesse James was actually dead. A little over a month after the incident, even Dr. Burns had been disabused. He admitted to a *Joplin Herald* reporter his role in treating Jim Cummins and surmised that one of the men who solicited his aid might have been Jesse James himself.

However, if Dr. Burns' initial report that the men told him they had seen a dead body being carried away is to be believed, it tends to lend credence to the opinion of those who suggested that the whole affray was arranged to make people think Jesse was dead. Another possibility, scarcely considered at the time of the incident, is that Shepherd sincerely thought he had killed Jesse and that the outlaw, having survived the attempted assassination, seized upon an opportunity to stage his own death. The fact is, though, that 130 years later no one seems much closer to the whole truth of the bizarre episode than Dr. Burns was in December of 1879.

11

Ozark Mountain Justice:
The Bald Knobbers of Southwest Missouri

In January of 1885, thirteen men, including Nat Kinney and other prominent citizens of Taney County, huddled in the back room of Yell Everett's store in Forsyth, Missouri, to talk about the rash of lawlessness plaguing their community. The Civil War had given rise in the bitterly divided state of Missouri to a brutal guerrilla conflict that often pitted neighbor against neighbor, and the violence it bred still persisted twenty years later.

Since the end of the war, nearly thirty murders had occurred in Taney County, and not one of the killers had been convicted of his crime. The final straw came in September of 1883 when Al Layton gunned down Yell Everett's brother Jim in a Forsyth saloon. Yell and his friends considered it cold-blooded murder, but just a couple of months before the back-room meeting, a sympathetic jury had declared Layton not guilty. All those assembled in Everett's store agreed something had to be done.

The men formed the Citizens' Committee to combat the rampant crime, and Nat Kinney, a giant of a man who stood about 6'5" and weighed nearly 250 pounds, took control of the meeting and assumed leadership of the group. A former Union soldier and Springfield saloonkeeper, Kinney had moved to Taney County two years earlier and started a Sunday school four miles south of Forsyth at the Oak Grove Schoolhouse, where he often railed against the social chaos and moral turpitude of his adopted county.

Kinney and his associates began recruiting other men to join the Citizens' Committee. Some balked when they learned the Law and Order League, as it was sometimes called, was to be an oath-sworn fraternity with secret signs, handshakes, and passwords. Many citizens, though, rushed

Nat Kinney, leader of the Bald Knobbers. (Courtesy Christian County Library)

to join up, and Kinney soon called a mass meeting to initiate the new recruits and organize the group.

Early on the morning of Sunday, April 5, 1885, more than one hundred men showed up at Snapp's Bald, a barren hill south of Forsyth near Kinney's farm, to be sworn into the vigilante society. Critics noted the forlorn meeting place with tongue in cheek and started calling members of the group Bald Knobbers, but the Citizens' Committee cheerfully adopted the name.

Word of the Knobbers' sunrise conclave caused mild excitement around Forsyth, but most folks took an amused, wait-and-see attitude. Nat Kinney knew it would take a bold, forceful act to show his group meant business and wouldn't tolerate any more legal shenanigans like those that had allowed Al Layton to go free. The following night, one hundred gun-toting Bald Knobbers with bandannas hiding their faces galloped into Forsyth and lined up around the jail in precise formation.

Young Newton Herrell, awaiting trial for the murder of his mother's lover back in October, saw the mob outside his cell and began screaming hysterically. The Bald Knobbers fetched the sheriff from his nearby home and demanded that he open

The slope near the top of the bald knob where the Bald Knobbers organized, as it appeared in the late 1800s. (Courtesy Christian County Library)

the jail door, but he refused and begged the mob not to carry through with their heinous plan. Perhaps they never intended to lynch Herrell or else they backed out when the sheriff resisted, because they simply draped a hangman's noose over the jail door and rode away into the night.

For citizens of Taney County, though, the Law and Order League now ceased to be a mere curiosity. The raid on the jail had gotten their attention, and people began choosing sides for or against the Bald Knobbers, mainly according to political sentiments left over from the Civil War. Old resentments died hard in the Ozarks hill country. The Bald Knobbers were mainly Republican former Union soldiers and sympathizers, while those opposed to the vigilante group tended to be Democratic ex-Confederates.

Among the Bald Knobbers' detractors were Frank and Tubal Taylor, a couple of local toughs with a reputation for rowdiness. The day after the jail incident, Frank stole a pair of boots from John T. Dickenson's store northeast of Forsyth after the merchant refused him credit. Dickenson, encouraged by the Bald Knobber meeting he had attended the previous Sunday, went to Forsyth on April 8 and swore out a warrant for Frank's arrest. The sheriff took the fugitive into custody but quickly released him on bond. Late the same day, Frank; his brother, Tubal; and another man went back to Dickenson's store to exact revenge. They shot Dickenson twice at point-blank range and fired a hail of bullets toward his wife. Then the desperadoes mounted up and rode away, leaving their victims for dead, but both survived.

The Taylors hid out in the rugged hills for about a week, and a $1,000 reward was offered for their capture. On April 14, they turned themselves in to friends who delivered them over to the sheriff. (The third man had fled the territory.) Frank and Tubal were jailed at Forsyth and indicted the following day on felonious assault charges. When a rumor spread that the brothers' surrender to their pals had been a mere scheme to collect their own reward, the Bald Knobbers flew into a rage.

About ten o'clock on the night of the fifteenth, one hundred riders, with kerchiefs covering their faces and their coats turned inside out, filed onto the Forsyth square and surrounded the jail much as they had a week and a half earlier. (In the meantime, Newton Herrell had been removed to Greene County.) Nat Kinney rode about the square ordering bystanders off the streets. Some of the Bald Knobbers appropriated a sledgehammer from a nearby blacksmith shop and started pounding on the jail's padlock with poor result. Kinney took the sledge and with three mighty blows sent the lock flying from the door, hinges and all.

The Knobbers stormed into the jail and pulled the kicking and screaming Taylors from their cell. The brothers were bound, placed aboard two horses, and carried to Swan Creek two miles northwest of town. Frank and Tubal wailed in protest as the unrelenting Knobbers strung them up to a big black oak tree and spanked the horses out from under them. The tightening nooses quickly choked off their pitiful howling. Someone fastened a crude sign to the front of Frank's shirt warning others to beware and signed it "THE BALD KNOBBERS." Then the mob turned and rode back toward Forsyth, leaving the bodies of Frank and Tubal Taylor swaying in the night air.

After the Taylor lynchings, loyalties in Taney County became more divided than ever. The Bald Knobbers faced increasing censure, and some of the original members dropped out of the group, appalled by what had taken place. Letters to the editor attacking the vigilantes began appearing in newspapers at Springfield and other towns throughout the state. A month or two after the hangings, a group of about thirty men, several of them Democratic, ex-county office holders who'd been ousted by Republicans in the previous election, formed the Anti-Bald Knobbers. At the same time, the Knobbers stepped up their recruiting efforts, and "Join the band or leave the land!" became their watchword. Some citizens did leave, and some who joined were unsavory characters who merely used the organization as a cover for their private escapades.

During the summer of 1885, Kinney and his missionaries gradually expanded their province from fighting crime to enforcing morality. Bands of night-riding crusaders roamed the countryside calling slackers or drunkards from their homes to be flogged for not supporting their families. Couples were driven off for living together without the stamp of matrimony. Squatters were expelled for not paying taxes. A party of midnight exhorters might visit the cabin of a backwoods Casanova whose gaze had lingered too long on a married woman, hail him with a shivaree of gunfire, and then warn him out of the county with a bundle of switches tossed in his doorway. The number of switches signified the number of days the would-be charmer had before he must leave the county or suffer the consequences.

Kinney's self-appointed role as arbiter of morality gained him as many critics as his more conspicuous deeds. Many old-time citizens did not consider "an ex-saloonkeeper from the slums of Springfield a proper censor of Taney County morals," as one local man stated it.

In December of 1885, the Taney County courthouse burned down, and charges and countercharges flew. The Bald Knobbers claimed the arson was an attempt by Anti-Bald Knobbers to destroy records to avoid paying taxes, while the latter group said it was another case of Knobber lawlessness.

Amidst this spirit of rancor, Andrew Coggburn and his friend Sam Snapp showed up at the Oak Grove School for Sunday evening church services on February 28, 1886. Coggburn's father had been killed in 1879 by men who later became Bald Knobbers, and the young man took great pride in ridiculing Nat Kinney and his "Sunday School crowd." The previous summer, he had tacked a miniature coffin to the schoolhouse door with a sign accusing Kinney of dispensing "pisen and death." He and his friends liked to imitate the "Old Blue Gobbler," their nickname for Kinney, by cackling like a turkey. He and Snapp had mocked the Bald Knobber rituals, and he and his brothers had been accused of disrupting religious services at Oak Grove. Young Coggburn often went about the countryside belting out a derisive song he had composed entitled "The Ballad of the Bald Knobbers." He had finally been charged with disturbing the peace, and Kinney had gotten himself deputized to execute the warrant.

When Coggburn and Snapp stepped outside at the end of church services, they were met by Kinney and a group of Bald Knobbers. Kinney drew his pistol, told Coggburn he was under arrest, and ordered him to raise his hands. According to the Bald Knobbers, Coggburn went for his gun instead, and Kinney shot him in the chest, killing him instantly. The next day a coroner's jury ruled the shooting self-defense. Snapp, the only witness who wasn't a Bald Knobber, claimed Coggburn was unarmed, but he had made a hasty getaway the night before and was too afraid to show up for the inquest.

The death of Andy Coggburn ignited a renewed public outcry against the Bald Knobbers. Hillbilly wordsmiths shot off bitter missives to Springfield newspapers, and even national newspapers started taking editorial stands against the Bald Knobbers. (The local *Taney County Home and Farm*, edited by Kinney's stepson, continued to support the vigilantes, of course.) The Anti-Bald Knobbers, after narrowly defeating a motion for open warfare, voted instead to form a local militia, and they petitioned Governor Marmaduke to arm the home-guard force and send in the state militia to help drive out the Bald Knobbers.

Marmaduke turned down the requests, but under increased pressure, he finally sent his adjutant general to persuade both the Bald Knobbers and the local militia group to disband. After some resistance to the idea, Kinney agreed. At a mass meeting on the courthouse lawn on April 10, 1886, with the state adjutant general in attendance, he formally announced the Bald Knobbers' dissolution.

Although the Knobbers and the local militia no longer existed as official organizations, the ill will spawned by the feud could not easily be laid aside. After the April 10 disbandment, the hostility between the two groups degenerated into a war of personal vendetta and a purging of old grudges.

Just a month later, on May 9, Kinney associate and part-time bodyguard Wash Middleton crossed paths with Sam Snapp on the front porch of Kintrea's General Store in Kirbyville, a small community five miles south of Forsyth. When Middleton heard Snapp humming Andy Coggburn's "Ballad of the Bald Knobbers," he called him a "damned bushwhacker," and a heated argument broke out. When Middleton pulled his revolver, Snapp threw up his hands and cried, "Don't!" Then he started backing away without going for his gun, but Middleton shot him three times.

The Anti-Bald Knobbers claimed Middleton had been hired by the Bald Knobbers to murder Snapp to keep him from testifying against Kinney in the shooting of Coggburn if the case ever went to trial. They vowed revenge but finally agreed to let the law take its course. Middleton was found guilty of second-degree murder, but he escaped (with the aid of Bald Knobbers, many said) and fled the territory. In 1888, detective Jim Holt, hired by the Snapp family to track the fugitive down, caught up with Middleton at Parthenon, Arkansas, and shot him dead at a Fourth of July picnic.

By the summer of 1886, vigilantism had spread from Taney to several surrounding counties. In 1885, Kinney had helped a group of men in neighboring Christian County organize a company of Bald Knobbers under the leadership of Dave Walker, a farmer who lived on Bull Creek in the eastern part of the county. The band did very little in its first year except develop an even more bizarre and esoteric set of rituals than its Taney County forerunner. For instance, each new recruit repeated a secret oath with a gun barrel pointed at his chest and a noose around his neck to emphasize the penalty of death that awaited those who broke the oath. The group also adopted masks of outlandish design that made the bandannas of the "Sunday School crowd" look benign.

After a year of relative inactivity, the Christian County Bald Knobbers went on a rampage. One Saturday afternoon, "Bull Creek Dave" and three hundred of his masked guardians of virtue rode into Chadwick, a railroad terminus with a

A sketch of John Matthews. (Courtesy Christian County Library)

reputation as a hell-hole of iniquity, and surrounded the saloon. They smashed the furniture, poured all the liquor into the streets, and sent a drunken customer home with a noose draped around his neck as a poignant reminder that drinking whiskey in a public house was not a suitable pastime for a family man. Throughout the summer, they roamed the Christian County countryside in their hideous

A sketch of Billy Walker. (Courtesy Christian County Library)

get-up administering discipline to backsliders and libertines. Anyone who dared complain or "talk agin the Bald Knobbers" was taught an edifying lesson with a cat o' nine tails.

On March 11, 1887, Dave Walker called a mass meeting on Bull Creek in a canyon called Smelter Holler north of Chadwick near the Bald Knobbers' secret cave for the ostensible purpose of disbanding the group because of the mounting criticism it had received. Dave's headstrong seventeen-year-old son William, though, was in no mood for capitulation. He vowed to whip William Edens, a young man who was suspected of being a member of the Slickers, an antivigilante group in the area. Edens had received a lashing once before for opposing the Bald Knobbers, and just that very day he had been heard suggesting that a Bald Knobber was no better than a sheep-killin' dog. So Billy Walker had little trouble recruiting several other Bald Knobbers, including Deacon John Matthews and his nephew Wiley Matthews, to help carry out his mission. When the meeting broke up, Billy and his cohorts cut several bundles of hickory switches and started after Edens, who lived on the Chadwick road not far from Smelter Holler. Dave Walker tagged along, vainly urging restraint.

The gang found young Edens spending the night at the nearby home of his father, James Edens. Also present were James's wife Elizabeth, William's wife Emma, William's sister Melvina, her husband Charles Green, and the latter couple's two small children. The Bald Knobbers pounded on the door

A sketch of John Matthews's cabin. (Courtesy Christian County Library)

and ordered William Edens outside, but before he could obey, one of the Knobbers opened fire through a window when he spotted Elizabeth Edens reaching for a gun. Several other masked men battered the doors down, burst into the house, and started shooting. The assault left William Edens and Charles Green dead, James Edens seriously wounded, and Melvina Green slightly injured. Before falling, Old Man Edens managed to get off one shot, wounding Billy Walker in the thigh.

Unlike in Taney County, the Bald Knobbers held no sway over local politics in Christian County. When word of the murders reached the county seat at Ozark seven miles to the west, Sheriff Zack Johnson and his deputies fanned out through the county and began rounding up Bald Knobbers left and right. Among those arrested and charged in the murders was Pastor C. O. Simmons of Chadwick, who two days earlier had conducted the funeral services for Edens and Green. As Ozarks folklorist Vance Randolph wryly observed years later, "Nearly all these murderers and outlaws, for some reason, were very religious men."

Alarmed by the seriousness of the charges against him, one young vigilante promptly broke his oath and started singing; several others soon joined the chorus in order to save their own skins. By late April of 1887, eighty men had been indicted on a variety of charges ranging from unlawful assembly to first-degree murder. Billy Walker, John Matthews, and Wiley Matthews were convicted of the most serious charge and sentenced to death. Dave Walker, the last to be tried on the first-degree murder charge, claimed he hadn't gone near the Edens' cabin on the fateful night and had even tried to stop the killings, but as leader of the Bald Knobbers he, too, was convicted and sentenced to join the other three on the gallows.

Wiley Matthews escaped and was never recaptured, but the other three were hanged simultaneously from a scaffold inside a stockade behind the Christian County jail at Ozark on May 10, 1889. The executions took a gruesome turn as

A *replica of a Bald Knobber mask at Christian County Museum.*

the noose around Billy Walker's neck jerked loose when he fell through the trapdoor. Witnesses inside the stockade turned away in horror as young Walker lay unconscious on the ground with blood seeping from his mouth, staining the hood that covered his face. As Walker regained consciousness, he started moaning pitifully and begging for deliverance. The mob of spectators outside the stockade shouted for him to be turned loose, but, with the help of the bystanding witnesses, Sheriff Johnson raised the boy back up and hanged him a second time. An attending doctor pronounced him dead thirty-four minutes after he, his father, and John Matthews had first dropped through the trapdoor.

Even as the round-up and imprisonment of Dave Walker and his followers was signaling the end of vigilantism in Christian County, the battle between Bald Knobbers and Anti-Bald Knobbers in Taney County flared up again. Local merchant and antivigilante James Berry filed for divorce from his wife and became embroiled with her lawyer, a friend of Nat Kinney, in a feud resulting in a wild exchange of gunfire on the Forsyth square on July 3, 1888.

Berry filed for bankruptcy in an attempt to keep his wife from gaining a share of the Berry Brothers store, but the merchant's ploy took an ironic turn when the judge appointed Nat Kinney as receiver of the merchandise. Berry made threats against Kinney, but the old Bald Knobber dismissed them as idle bluster and took charge of the inventory. On Monday morning, August 20, 1888, Kinney was in the store invoicing goods when Berry appeared on the other side of the square with a rifle crooked under his arm. However, it was a mere posture to decoy Kinney's Bald Knobber friends while Berry's pals Billy and Jim Miles entered the store.

Billy Miles had won the assignment of killing Kinney at a secret Anti-Bald Knobber meeting months before and had been biding his time awaiting a favorable opportunity to carry it out. Recently, he had worked at Berry's store before the bankruptcy, but after Kinney took charge of the inventory, he had ordered the twenty-one-year-old Miles to stay away. As Miles walked over to inspect a pair of shoes, Kinney again ordered him out and reached for his pistol on a nearby shelf, but Miles beat him to the draw. He jerked a .44 Smith and Wesson from his holster and filled the "Old Blue Gobbler" with lead.

Billy Miles was charged with murder but was bailed out by friends. While Billy was awaiting trial in the Kinney case, Taney County sheriff Galba Branson and an Arkansas man named Ed Funk, whom antivigilantes claimed had been hired to avenge Kinney's death, tracked the parolee down at an Independence Day celebration at Kirbyville in 1889 and forced a showdown. Billy and his brothers, Jim and Emanuel, killed both the hired gunman and the ex-Bald Knobber sheriff in the Fourth of July fireworks. A jury later ruled that Billy had acted in self-defense in the Kinney case, and he and his brother Jim were also acquitted in the Branson case. Emanuel was never tried.

In March of 1892, a drunken horde burst into the Forsyth jail and dragged a wife murderer named John Wesley Bright from his cell. They shot and killed a deputy sheriff in the process, then hanged Bright from a tree at a nearby cemetery. The tragedy stands as the last instance of vigilantism in Taney County. However, it was more the spontaneous behavior of an unruly mob than the deliberate action of an organized vigilante group.

BALD KNOBBER COUNTRY

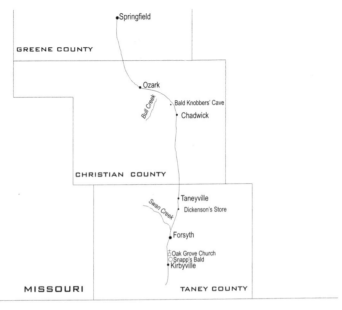

Map of Bald Knobber country.

Without Nat Kinney's leadership, Bald Knobberism had already become a thing of the past, and during the years that followed, the intense hatreds and prejudices that gave rise to the movement gradually subsided. Even today in the Ozarks region, though, one can still find people with strong opinions about the Bald Knobbers, especially among those whose forefathers were prominent players in the turbulent drama acted out on the Christian and Taney County stage more than one hundred years ago.

12

Emma Molloy and the Most Sensational Murder Case in Greene County History

After George Graham bigamously married Cora Lee, foster daughter of nationally known temperance revivalist Emma Molloy, in the summer of 1885 and then killed his first wife and stashed her body in an abandoned well at Molloy's Brookline farm, a Springfield newspaper headline called the murder the "blackest and most fiendish known in the Southwest." Graham's lynching by a mob at Springfield the following spring before he could be tried for the crime only added to the sensationalism surrounding the case. In addition, the preliminary hearing of Cora Lee and Emma Molloy as accessories to the murder became a scandalous spectacle that drew hundreds of curious onlookers, hungry for lurid details. Almost thirty years later, historians Jonathan Fairbanks and Clyde Edwin Tuck still considered the crime "perhaps the most cruel murder in the history of Greene County," and they called the hearing of the two women "the most spectacular court procedure in the entire life of the county."

Emma Molloy was already well-known as an author, evangelist, and speaker in the Women's Christian Temperance Union movement when she, accompanied by Cora Lee, came to Springfield in the winter of 1884-85. She held a series of revival meetings at the First Congregational Church, located at the northeast corner of Jefferson and Locust Streets. Before the meetings were over, thirty-five-year-old George E. Graham arrived in town and started wooing twenty-three-year-old Cora Lee. Graham was an ex-convict whom Mrs. Molloy had befriended years before, and he had recently been associated with her at Washington, Kansas, in the publication of a Prohibition newspaper called *The Morning and Day of Reform.*

MRS. EMMA MOLLOY, THE REVIVALIST AND REFORMER.

Newspaper sketch of Emma Molloy

After the series of revivals ended, Emma Molloy, with the assistance of prominent Springfield citizen Judge James Baker, purchased a farm about five miles west of Springfield near Brookline. The forty-six-year-old Mrs. Molloy, Cora Lee, George Graham, an adopted daughter of Mrs. Molloy, and a second foster daughter took up residence there. Graham had married his first wife, Sarah, in 1871, and she had divorced him after he went to prison for horse stealing two years later. Although the couple had reunited after his release, Graham apparently succeeded in convincing Mrs. Molloy and Miss Lee that he and Sarah had never rewed. He and Cora were married in Springfield on July 18, 1885.

Shortly afterwards, Mrs. Molloy left Springfield to hold another series of revival meetings. While she was gone, Graham summoned his first wife at Fort Wayne, Indiana, to bring their two boys, ages thirteen and six, to St. Louis, where he planned to meet her and take the boys on to Brookline to live with him. Sarah showed up in St. Louis as scheduled, but, instead of turning her sons over to her estranged husband, she accompanied him and the two children to Springfield on September 30.

Leaving the boys with an acquaintance in Springfield, Graham took Sarah to the Brookline farm. On the late night of September 30 or early morning on October 1, he killed her, perhaps to keep her from finding out about his marriage to Cora Lee. After shooting her in the chest, he dumped her body in an abandoned well on the farm. Graham later told his eldest son, Charlie, that he had left Sarah in Springfield but that Charlie should say, if asked, that they had left his mother in St. Louis.

Around Christmas of 1885, law officers in Greene County began receiving letters of inquiry from family members in Fort Wayne concerning the welfare and whereabouts of Sarah Graham. Shortly after the first of the New Year, Constable O'Neil of Brookline talked to George Graham and asked him where Sarah was. Graham told the lawman that the last time he had seen her was the day he had left her at the Union Depot in St. Louis.

Graham knew now, though, that the law was on his trail, and he began making plans to flee the area. He passed two or three forged checks at a Springfield bank to get money to leave, but before he could depart, the bankers spotted the deception. However, Emma Molloy, who was temporarily back home, made restitution for him, and the matter was dropped. A few days later, Constable O'Neil spoke to Mrs. Molloy about Sarah Graham's whereabouts, and Mrs. Molloy told him she thought Sarah was staying at a house of ill repute in St. Louis. Shortly afterwards, Mrs. Molloy left again to conduct a series of meetings at Peoria, Illinois.

Toward the end of January, T. L. Breese, Sarah Graham's brother-in-law, arrived from Fort Wayne to look for Sarah. Upon learning that George Graham was married to Cora Lee, Breese preferred a charge of bigamy against Graham, because Graham's second marriage to Sarah had never been dissolved. On January 29, Graham was arrested on the charge and incarcerated in the Greene County jail.

Breese, Constable O'Neil, and another Brookline resident called at the Molloy farm in early February to investigate Sarah Graham's disappearance but were turned away by Cora Lee. Feeling that Breese's sister-in-law had been "foully dealt with," the citizens around Brookline, however, persisted in their determination to search the Molloy premises. On February 25, a party of men instituted a thorough search and found Sarah's nude and partially decomposed body at the bottom of an old, abandoned well on the farm.

George Graham, still being held in jail on the bigamy charge, was now charged with murder, while Emma Molloy was charged with being an accessory after the fact and Cora Lee with being an accessory before the fact. Cora Lee was immediately arrested, and Mrs. Molloy was arrested in early March upon her return from Peoria. Both women were held in the Polk County jail at Bolivar.

When the preliminary hearing for the women began on March 12, a standing-room-only crowd jammed the Greene County courthouse "eager to catch a glimpse of the

SPRINGFIELD. MO., FRIDAY MORNI

A HORRIBLE STORY!

The Mystery of the Disappearance
of Mrs. Sarah Graham
Cleared by

The Discovery of Her Dead and Murdered Body on the Molloy
Farm.

Found in the Bottom of a Well
Sixty Feet Deep
With a

Bullet Hole in the Breast—Greene
County the Scene of
the Most

Wanton Murder Ever Recorded
in the Annals of
Crime.

Circumstances Point to George E.
Graham as the Slayer of
His Wife.

hysicians

ARE

L. McELHANY
Cashier.

Bank,

), MO.
ED 1867

special at-

In introducing tes
the 28th of last
appointment, met
Louis, where she
the two children.
tered at the Cer
Graham, wife an
remained in St. L
and on the mornin
party took the tra
which all trace of
was lost. The cl
in this examinatic
of his mother sh
depot platform i
bearing himself, i
father moved aw:
enced in this tes
statement made
publish in this co
The Justice co
sufficiently strong
for bigamy, and
GRAHAM WA
in the county jai
loary examination
Ft. Wayne, Ind
mysteriously mis
ent, and thorou
wife's sister had
be assisted energ
tion for bigamy th
Graham securely
investigation as
the missing wo
that the interest

Headlines in a Springfield newspaper tell the story of Sarah Graham's murder.

prisoners." Seeking to show that Cora Lee and Emma Molloy were dissolute women capable of abetting and covering up a murder, the prosecutors introduced highly scandalous, although dubious, testimony. Graham's son Charlie, for instance, said that he had seen his father, Cora Lee, and Emma Molloy share the same bed on several occasions. No doubt trying to diffuse some of the blame for the murder of his wife, Graham himself gave a statement from his jail cell that was published by the press. He claimed, among other things, that he had been having intimate relations for more than three years with both Cora Lee and the twice-divorced Emma Molloy. At the conclusion of the hearing on March 31, both women were bound over for trial. Cora Lee was held without bail, and Emma Molloy was released on $5,000 bond.

Almost a month later, George Graham had still not been indicted, and his lawyers were seeking a writ of habeas corpus to get him released when an angry mob took matters into their own hands. Shortly before 2:00 A.M. on April 27, a party of men numbering between 100 and 150, nearly all of them armed and wearing masks, converged on the public square, most of them riding in from the west along College Street. Halting their horses in front of the courthouse and jail near the northwest corner of the square, several of them dismounted and barged into the jail. They placed Sheriff F. M. Donnell and a watchman under guard, took the jail keys, and located Graham in his cell. After rousing him and ordering him to get dressed, they wrapped a noose around his neck and, forcing the watchman to accompany them, led the prisoner outside. They placed him in a horse-drawn wagon and started off down Boonville Avenue. Turning west, they took him to an area near Grant Beach Park and stopped at a scrub oak tree. With a noosed Graham still in the wagon, they made him stand up and tied the rope to an overhanging branch. They asked Graham if he had any last words, and he said he loved his kids and that both Cora Lee and Emma Molloy were entirely innocent. Then the mob drove the wagon out from under him. With his feet almost touching the ground, Graham clung to life for twenty-one minutes.

Around 5:00 A.M., the watchman returned to the scene with Sheriff Donnell, and they cut the body down. Pinned to the dead man's back was a notice proclaiming the right of "the three hundred" to take the law into their own hands in this case and "remove from our midst the worst criminal who has ever infested our country." The notice also warned that anyone who tried to "discover the actors in this tragedy will be surely and speedily dispatched to hell, where all things are revealed to the curious."

The authors of the note subscribed themselves "in justice to the memory of Sarah Graham . . . whose life was sacrificed at the altar of Hecate," and they signed the note, "Citizens of Greene County, Mo." Then, in a dire postscript, they warned Sheriff Donnell, "Keep your mouth shut if you recognized any of us or you will die the death of a dog."

Later in the day, a coroner's inquest was held, and the jury determined that "George E. Graham came to his death by being hung by the neck until dead by parties to this jury unknown."

A letter that Graham had sent to a local newspaper a few days earlier with instructions that it not be opened without his permission was unsealed after his death. It contained a statement corroborating his dying declaration that Cora Lee and Emma Molloy were innocent.

On May 10, Mrs. Molloy issued her own public statement, published by a Springfield newspaper, in which she declared her innocence. She claimed her only fault had been in trusting George Graham too much and said many of the slanderous allegations made against her were a result of her status as a noted female temperance lecturer. "There are no two classes of people whom the world . . . so readily believe a scandal about as a minister of the gospel and a woman, but when the two characters are combined, and a scandal can be concocted sufficiently ingenious for the public to swallow, however nauseating and polluting it may be, it is devoured with an ecstasy of delight."

About this time, Cora Lee was also released on bond, and the two women left town. Two months later, still reeling from the humiliation of the Graham case, Emma Molloy suffered an even greater emotional blow when her son and only biological child died by drowning.

In June of 1887, Cora Lee returned to Springfield to stand

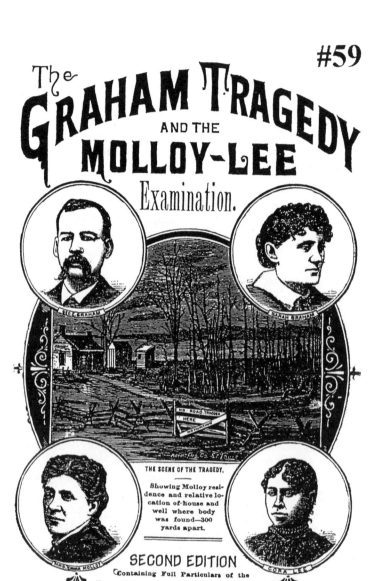

The front page of a sensationalist tract about events surrounding the murder of Sarah Graham, originally published approximately a year after the murder.

trial, and the jury, pondering much the same evidence that had been presented at the preliminary hearing the previous year, could not reach a verdict. Meanwhile, charges against Mrs. Molloy were dropped. Then in January of 1888, Cora Lee was retried and acquitted. Both women were thus cleared of any wrongdoing in the Graham murder case; however, the taint of scandal lingered.

Emma Molloy gradually recovered from the heartache of her son's death and the embarrassment of the Graham case. During the 1890s, she went on to conduct a series of highly successful revivals on the West Coast and to reestablish herself as one of the most prominent temperance evangelists in the country. She died in 1907.

Many startling crimes, such as the Young brothers' massacre of the early 1930s, have occurred in the Springfield area since Fairbanks and Tuck suggested ninety years ago that the Sarah Graham murder case was the most spectacular in the history of Greene County, but one would be hard pressed to refute their claim even today. The Graham case, because of the Victorian age in which it occurred and the prominent status of one of the principals involved, remains unsurpassed and perhaps unequaled in the sensation it aroused. As Emma Molloy pointed out herself, the public loved nothing better during the nineteenth century than to see a woman or a minister disgraced, and Mrs. Molloy happened to be both.

13

Barry County's Most Shocking Crime

When Ed Clum came to Missouri in the summer of 1885 and visited the J. J. White farm in northern Barry County, he let it be known to hired hands on the property that he and White were old acquaintances from New York, White's ailing wife was his sister, and he was there to take her to Lebanon to stay with another sister. To the workers, Clum and White were not only brothers-in-law, but also appeared to be good friends. Neighbors and family back east, though, knew the real story.

Both Clum and White were from Wayne County, New York, had served in the same company during the Civil War, and had remained close after the war. To local observers, their alliance seemed an odd one. The families of both men were well thought of in the community, but White was considered more intelligent and more polished than his friend. He had married around 1862 when he was about twenty-three years old. His wife, Augusta Wyman, came from a prominent family and was considered a refined young lady. Clum, on the other hand, had been rebellious even as a boy and after the war had led a dissolute life, earning a reputation as a brute. In 1869, when he was twenty-five, he married a seventeen-year-old girl named Charlotte, also known as Lottie, whose recklessness matched his own.

White's one failing seemed to be his careless attitude toward women. He had long been known as being "partial to ladies' society," but around 1880 when he and Clum settled on farms close to each other near the village of West Walworth, he started engaging in drunken debauches with the neighboring couple and openly pursuing Mrs. Clum. Lottie Clum soon earned a reputation as a "common prostitute" and Jay White was thought a "slick villain," while Ed Clum's failure to put a stop to the shenanigans between White and his wife excited equal disgust from disapproving neighbors.

In 1883, both families moved to nearby Fairport in neighboring Monroe County, where Clum worked as a foreman on a railroad contract and White briefly served as his supervisor on the same job. White and Clum joined the Fairport post of the Grand Army of the Republic (GAR) together, but White shortly afterwards got himself kicked out for riding a horse up and down the streets of Fairport in the company of Mrs. Clum, with both of them in a "beastly state of intoxication" and endangering the lives of pedestrians. The scandal arising from White's philandering with Mrs. Clum was the gossip of the community, and it became more than Mrs. White could take. She committed suicide on Memorial Day of 1884 by hanging herself from a balustrade in her Fairport home, mainly, it was thought, because of the shame her husband had brought on her and her family. White was away on a business trip when news of the tragedy reached him, but when he got home, instead of observing a period of mourning, he went immediately to his neighbor's house and got drunk with Mr. and Mrs. Clum.

Around this time, Clum was arrested for stealing sheep and other property, and White strengthened the considerable sway he already enjoyed over the younger, coarser man when he helped Clum avoid the penitentiary by negotiating a deal in which Clum agreed to turn state's evidence. White also persuaded Clum to move away, apparently as part of the deal to keep him out of jail. Clum relocated to the nearby city of Rochester with the understanding that his wife would soon join him, but she stayed behind long enough for her relationship with White to grow even more intimate. When she finally joined her husband in Rochester, where he was working as a butcher, she was in ill health. She and Clum agreed in the spring of 1885 that she should go to stay with a sister in Lebanon, Missouri, where it was thought the change in climate might do her good.

About the same time, presumably by predesign with Mrs. Clum, White also migrated to Missouri, leaving behind a grown son, a teenage daughter, and a four-year-old girl.

During the first week of May, he bought a farm about five miles south of Pierce City (spelled Peirce City at the time) on Capps Creek near the village of Pulaskifield. After securing the land, he promptly visited Lottie Clum at Lebanon and brought her back with him to his Barry County farm.

Now, two months later, Ed Clum had learned from Lottie's sister that his wife had left Lebanon. After a hurried trip from New York, he showed up at the farm to take his wife back to her sister's house, but while there, he went along with the lie White and Lottie had constructed, introducing himself as Lottie's brother, presumably to protect her reputation. After a brief stay at the farm, he and Lottie boarded an eastbound train, and, eliciting a promise from her that she would follow as soon as she felt well enough to complete the journey, he dropped Lottie off at Lebanon and went back home to Rochester.

Instead of joining her husband in New York, Lottie returned with White to his farm. However, when her health continued to fail, she wrote Clum asking him to come after her. He returned to Missouri a second time in the latter part of 1885 and again took her to Lebanon. She was supposed to wait a few days for her sister, who was to accompany her to New York, but she again returned to White's farm.

Meanwhile, Clum went home and got himself booted out of the GAR at Fairport just as his friend and rival had done earlier. On September 27, 1885, he was dishonorably discharged for showing up drunk at a campout sponsored by the post and using vile and obscene language in the presence of the other members' wives and daughters.

In February of 1886, Clum received word that his wife had died on January 25, and shortly afterwards, he again started for Missouri over the objections of his parents and other family members. Arriving in early March, he moved in with White and resumed the charade he had begun during his earlier visits, pretending to be the brother of White's deceased wife. Clum and White often made trips to Pierce City together to get supplies, and casual observers in the community considered them the best of friends.

Also living in the household were Mrs. Olive Vassar, whom White had hired as a housekeeper the previous December, and her fourteen-year-old son, Thomas "Buddy" Vassar. Willis Dehoney, a twenty-five-year-old black hired hand, lived on the farm in a separate house with his wife. The previous fall, White had also employed Ella Bowe, daughter of a neighboring farmer, to cook and, while Lottie was still alive, to help take care of his "wife" on occasion.

The seventeen-year-old girl continued to make frequent trips to White's home during 1886, and she and White spent an increasing amount of time together. Clum could not have failed to notice that his old rival was taking more than a passing interest in the young girl. Some reports suggest that the squat, red-faced Clum had taken a fancy to the girl himself and was jealous because she favored the taller, handsomer White. Even discounting such a motive, though, Clum had ample reason to resent the budding relationship between the couple. Especially after he talked to the housekeeper.

Mrs. Vassar looked askance on her employer's dalliance with a seventeen-year-old girl, and as she got to know Ed Clum, she began to speak her mind to him on the subject. Sometime around July 1, 1886, she told Clum she felt White had maltreated his (Clum's) "sister" by carrying on with Ella Bowe right under Lottie's nose. *The same way he carried on with Lottie right under my nose,* Clum must have thought bitterly. Mrs. Vassar said Ella was present and helped White attend to Lottie on the night she died, and the housekeeper even intimated that the two had dosed Lottie with some sort of powder that might have hastened her death. Mrs. Vassar told Clum that on the day of Lottie's funeral, White and Ella came back to the farm together after the service in a state of intoxication. The housekeeper said Ella had told her that she and Mr. White were planning to get married.

Ed Clum had heard enough. White had made him a cuckold and a laughing stock before, but this time Clum meant to get the last laugh. In the late afternoon of July 8, he took White's double-barrel, breech-loading shotgun and marched along the edge of a wheat field behind the farmhouse toward Capps Creek, where White and Ella were lounging beneath a walnut tree. Willis Dehoney was in the field loading lodged wheat onto a wagon, and he called Clum over to help him. Muttering and cursing, Clum walked over, helped load the wagon, and told Dehoney threateningly, "I am going to do something that you don't know anything about."

As Dehoney drove the loaded wagon toward the barn, Clum tramped along behind him following the creek and carrying the shotgun. When Dehoney was about seventy yards beyond the bend in the creek where White and Ella Bowe were lazing beneath the walnut tree, he looked back and saw Clum stop beside the tree and suddenly point the gun in the direction where the lovers were sitting. Clum fired both barrels of the shotgun in quick succession, reloaded rapidly, and fired both barrels again. The two victims died almost instantly. White's fatal wound was a shot to the forehead and Ella's was a load of buckshot in the small of the back.

Clum reloaded a second time and turned to Dehoney. Beckoning the hired man with a wave of his hand, he yelled for him to turn around and come back. Clum forced the

Headstone of Ella Bowe beside her mother's at St. Patrick's Cemetery in Pierce City.

hired hand to help him cover the bodies with some of the straw from the wagon. The two men then started toward the barn together and met Buddy Vassar along the way. At the barn, as the three started toward their houses to eat supper, Clum told Dehoney to meet him back at the barn in thirty minutes if he wanted to live.

Fearing for his life, Dehoney did as he was told, and later that evening, he helped Clum move the bodies to a blind ditch in a field not far from where the couple was killed. The two men covered the bodies with rocks, dirt, and straw. On their way back to the barn aboard the wagon, Clum told the hired man, "Willis . . ., if you ever whimper this or I ever think you are making arrangements on this earth, I expect to put a ball plumb through you." At another point, Clum reached over and laid his hand on Dehoney's shoulder. "Willis, that little woman that died here last winter was my wife," he said. Then he was silent, as though nothing else needed to be said on the subject.

For almost two weeks, Dehoney was too afraid to try to tell anybody what he knew. When Mrs. Vassar inquired about White and Miss Bowe, Clum told her they had gone to Springfield to get married. Finally, on July 19, using the ruse that he was sick and needed to go to town for medicine, Dehoney slipped away to Pierce City and told Chief of Police R. J. Chappell what had happened. Chappell and a citizen named Stellhorn went out to the White farm and arrested Clum without resistance. He was lodged overnight in the Pierce City jail. The next day, he was turned over to the Barry County sheriff and transported to the county jail at Cassville. The bodies of White and Miss Bowe were uncovered the same day Clum was arrested, and an inquest was held the following day.

At his trial in circuit court at Cassville in September, Clum was found guilty of first-degree murder and sentenced to death by hanging. Had he killed White in New York a few years earlier, as the editor of his hometown newspaper suggested, "A jury could not have been found to convict him

The old Pierce City jail, where Clum was first incarcerated, as it appears today.

The hanging of Ed Clum in Cassville on April 15, 1887, was well attended. (Courtesy Fields' Photo Archives)

of murder," but he had crossed the line when he directed his vengeance at a love-struck, seventeen-year-old girl. The execution was originally scheduled for November, but an appeal to the Missouri Supreme Court postponed it until the following spring. On the day Clum was scheduled to hang, April 15, 1887, several people, including a couple of ministers, visited him in his cell during the morning and early afternoon. Hymns were sung, and prayers were offered. Clum asked to have Lottie's ashes reinterred with him after his death. "She was untrue to me," he said, "but I would have forgiven her and taken her back, because I loved her."

At midafternoon, Clum was escorted from his cell to a scaffold that had been erected not far from the courthouse square. He talked freely with his escorts and to those on and near the gallows; he asked a friend from Walworth, who had traveled from New York, to tell his parents he had gone to Jesus. Then, as the appointed moment drew near, Clum fell silent and met his fate with a stoic face. At precisely 3:07 P.M., he was launched into eternity before five to ten thousand curious spectators who'd turned out to view the execution of the man who had perpetrated what was called at the time "Barry County's most shocking crime."

14

The Blalock-Fry Gang of Southeast Kansas

After John and William Blalock shot and killed Constable David Gordon on the grounds of a nursery in Columbus, Kansas, late on the night of March 16, 1888, they crossed the road to their home, where they were met by their mother, Ellen, who had been awakened by the gunshots. When Mrs. Blalock asked her sons what the shooting was all about, John told her he and Bill had killed "some goddamn son of a bitch prowling around in front of the house."

Upon hearing the news, Mrs. Blalock "made considerable fuss about it," but John told her Gordon would have killed them if they hadn't killed him, because they had heard him cock his pistol and saw him start toward them. Apparently satisfied by the explanation, the mother fed the boys and handed Bill some money she had been holding for him. Afterwards, the brothers changed clothes and left.

Gordon's murder was the climax of a string of crimes throughout 1887 and the spring of 1888 that had aroused the folks in and around Columbus to a state of alarm. In January of 1887, a lap robe, some shoes, and other belongings were taken from the home of a local man named Fred Basom, and his house was doused with coal oil and set on fire. In late May of the same year, a Frisco Railroad car was broken open and robbed in Columbus. A month later Basom, was mysteriously shot and wounded at the south edge of town by what was considered stray gunfire at the time. Later that summer, the post office and store at nearby Sherwin was robbed. Several other homes and businesses, including a hardware store and a jewelry store in Columbus, were burglarized throughout the year.

After a lull of a few months, the crimes resumed in early 1888 at an even faster pace than before. In early March, the train depot at Crestline, a neighboring village, was broken into and robbed. A week later, a store at Lowell, another area community, was robbed. Citizens of Cherokee County grew increasingly worried as it became ever clearer that a gang of outlaws dwelt in their very midst.

Suspicion gradually settled on the Blalock and Fry families of Columbus. Besides twenty-eight-year-old John and twenty-six-year-old William, the Blalocks consisted of the father, the mother, one other adult son, and five daughters. The old man, fifty-three-year-old Oliver C. Blalock, had spent a number of years in an insane asylum and had only recently been released. John had spent a couple of years in jail for stealing cattle ten years earlier when he was just a lad, and shortly after his release, he and William had been named in a lawsuit by a woman who claimed the pair had swindled her out of a brace of mules. One of the daughters, eighteen-year-old Clara, however, was a local schoolteacher with an excellent reputation in the community. The Fry family consisted of the old man, the mother, three adult sons, and at least three daughters. A male cousin, twenty-one-year-old Grant Alley, was also staying with the family part time. The father, Andrew Fry, was unemployed because, according to one of his daughters, it was "very dull here for men to

Mrs. Mary Fry, mother of the Fry brothers, worked at this hotel on the square in Columbus. (Courtesy Cherokee County Genealogical and Historical Society)

get work," and the family had an unsavory reputation that rivaled that of the Blalocks. The Blalock sons and the Fry boys were known cohorts, and it was thought they were working together as part of an organized gang.

When the latest crime spurt in March of 1888 coincided with the return of the young men to Columbus after a period of absence, the two families came under mounting scrutiny. Then, when the safe at the Kansas City, Fort Scott & Gulf Railroad depot in Columbus was blown open and robbed of $360 on the evening of March 15, just one night after the robbery at the Lowell store, suspicion rested squarely on the Blalocks and Frys. Cherokee County sheriff Jim Babb dispatched Constable Gordon the next evening, March 16, to the Blalock neighborhood at the south edge of Columbus to keep an eye on the comings and goings of the family.

The Blalock brothers spent the evening of the sixteenth at the Fry residence in the southwest part of Columbus. Meanwhile, Gordon took up his lookout behind a small hedge at a nursery across the street from the Blalock home. All was quiet for the first couple of hours. Shortly before midnight, the Blalocks started for home with John carrying a Winchester rifle and Bill toting a shotgun loaded with double-ought shot.

As the brothers neared their house, Bill spotted the shadowy figure of a man on the grounds of the nursery and pointed him out to John. The two stopped in the road, and John called out to the man, asking him what he wanted. When the only answer was the cocking of a pistol, John fired his rifle. The man started running, and a single blast from Bill's shotgun brought the fleeing figure down. "Don't shoot," Gordon yelled as he fell. "I'm badly shot." The Blalocks went over to check on the man, but he was dead by the time they got there. Bill recognized him as Dave Gordon. Leaving the body where it was, they crossed the street to their house and told their mother what had happened.

Now, as they were leaving the house, they went back over to check on Gordon again, with a lantern they had gotten at home. Finding him still dead, they walked downtown, then started along the road west of Columbus. A few miles outside town, they turned south and spent the next day, Saturday, March 17, holed up in a rural schoolhouse.

Meanwhile, Gordon's body was discovered on Saturday morning across the road from the Blalock home, and the suspicion that had previously been directed toward the family turned to a firm conviction that they were somehow involved in the recent spate of crimes, including Gordon's death. Mr. and Mrs. Blalock and their daughters were held as witnesses, and a search warrant was issued for the Blalock home. The sheriff found a cache of stolen property and a number of letters that "proved to be a bonanza in the way of fixing guilt upon the outfit."

The same morning a coroner's jury was impaneled to hold an inquest into Gordon's death. Clara Blalock was called as the first witness, and she positively denied any knowledge of Gordon's death or of the whereabouts of her brothers. Confronted with some of the letters found at her home, most of which were addressed to her by a party using a seemingly fictitious name and many of which referred to criminal activities, she denied any knowledge of what the letters meant or who the actual writer was. (The writer later proved to be her brother John.) Two of her younger sisters were also called to testify, and they, too, denied any knowledge of criminal activity.

On Saturday evening, Clara and her mother finally agreed to tell the whole truth if they could be protected from prosecution. Clara was granted immunity and her mother leniency in return for their testimony. Ellen Blalock told all she knew about the circumstances of Gordon's death, and Clara revealed details of many of the crimes that had been committed in the area during the past couple of years. She implicated her brothers John and Bill, the Frys, and others and even incriminated herself as the "secretary" of the gang.

On Sunday, John and Bill Blalock walked back toward Columbus and sneaked up to their house. Noticing it was under guard, they retreated several miles southwest of town and took shelter in another rural schoolhouse. They decided the lower part of the building was not a secure hideout, so they climbed on top of the schoolhouse and sawed a hole in the roof to gain access to the attic. A young man passing by, however, heard the sawing and saw the shadowy figure of a man in front of the schoolhouse. Suspecting the men at the schoolhouse could be the Blalocks, he continued on and told the farmer he lived with what he had witnessed.

When the farmer came to Columbus early Monday morning and reported the young man's statement, a posse organized and went out to the schoolhouse. Noticing the pole the Blalocks had used to shinny on top of the schoolhouse, one of the men climbed a ladder to the roof and discovered the Blalocks' hideout covered by a crude trapdoor made of shingles. He knocked the door off before climbing back down. The posse then shouted to the occupants of the schoolhouse that they had been discovered and demanded their surrender. The Blalocks agreed to come out if they wouldn't be shot. Assured they would be protected, they came out with their hands up, leaving their firearms in the attic. One of the posse members retrieved the weapons, and the pair was escorted to Columbus and lodged in the county

Early-day Columbus (Courtesy Cherokee County Genealogical and Historical Society)

jail before most of the townspeople knew of their arrest.

The coroner's inquest had resumed on Monday morning and was in noon recess when word reached the courthouse square that the brothers were in jail just down the street. Shouts went up, and some in the crowd of a hundred men yelled for Judge Lynch to "hang 'em." The mayor and other town dignitaries, however, advised the crowd to let the law take its course. One of the posse members reminded them that the Blalocks had surrendered peacefully when they probably could have killed every member of the posse if they had wanted to put up a fight. He said the posse had given their word that the captives would be protected, and they meant to keep their word. The mob gradually calmed down and overwhelmingly agreed, on a show of hands, to support the law officers and court officials.

Bill Blalock was promptly marched from the jail to testify before the coroner's jury. His testimony corroborated and expanded upon that given earlier by his sister and mother. He either confessed to or implicated other members of the Blalock-Fry gang in nearly all the burglaries and robberies that had taken place in Cherokee County during recent years, and he admitted that he and John had killed Constable Gordon "because he was watching our house."

John Blalock then came before the jury and gave much the same testimony his brother had offered. He said he had "been in the business of robbing . . . about three years." He admitted, among numerous other crimes, burning down a beehive factory in Columbus because he "was mad at everybody for the hard luck I was in and the rough time I saw." Others testifying before the jury included Mr. and Mrs. Fry and three Fry sisters. One of the sisters, eighteen-year-old Helen, said she had tried to talk her brothers out of "yanking" other people's property but that they had told her they "didn't give a damn" and planned to keep on stealing.

On March 19, the same day Bill and John Blalock testified, their brother, Clay, was arrested in Abilene, Kansas, but he was later released after it was concluded he'd had nothing to do with the gang's exploits. The following day, two of the Fry brothers, Alex and Dan, were arrested in Fayetteville, Arkansas, and brought back to Columbus.

At their preliminary hearings in early May, the principals in the gang pled guilty to a variety of crimes. John and Bill Blalock were sentenced to life in prison for murder and robbery. Their mother got three years for receiving stolen property, while Clara received immunity for her testimony. Alex Fry, who was considered the leader of the Fry part of the gang, received fifteen years for burglary. His younger brother, Dan, got sixteen years. Another brother, Fred, or "Ped" as he was usually called, got six years for his minor involvement in the gang's activities, while the father was sentenced to five years for receiving and concealing stolen property. The cousin, Grant Alley, received thirteen years.

John Blalock died in prison in 1899. His mother, released after a couple of years in prison, came back to Columbus and died at the age of sixty-two in 1901, two years before her husband. A prison guard shot Bill Blalock when he tried to escape in 1896, but he recovered from his wound and was pardoned in 1908. He went to live with his sister Clara in Wisconsin, where he worked as a shoe cobbler until his death in 1915. All the Frys served their time and were released.

A newspaperman claimed at the time of the Blalock-Fry gang's arrest that they were "one of the worst murderous and thieving gangs that has ever infested any country." While this was a fine piece of exaggeration, the gang's notorious reputation was the talk of the day throughout southeast Kansas back in 1888, and 120 years later, their story is still a local legend.

15

The Dalton Gang's Waterloo at Coffeyville

Bob Dalton had big ideas as he and the other members of his gang rode toward Coffeyville, Kansas, on the early morning of October 5, 1892. He had grown up admiring his infamous cousins, the Youngers, and their notorious sidekicks, Frank and Jesse James. Merely emulating the James-Younger gang, though, wasn't enough for Bob Dalton, who had recently stated that he meant to "lower the record of Jesse James."

The plan was to ride into town and rob the Condon Bank and the nearby First National Bank simultaneously. Not even the James and Youngers had ever attempted such an audacious feat as robbing two banks at once. There was one thing Bob Dalton didn't count on: the citizens of Coffeyville.

Besides twenty-three-year-old ringleader Bob Dalton, the outlaw gang included Bob's older brother Grat, his younger brother Emmett, Dick Broadwell, and Bill Power. Another Dalton brother, Frank, had been a deputy U. S. marshal until he was killed in 1887 in the line of duty, and his three brothers had briefly followed in his footsteps as lawmen before turning to horse thievery. By 1891, they had graduated to train robbery, and by the fall of 1892, they had already made a name for themselves as notorious outlaws. Deputy Marshal Heck Thomas was close on their trail, and Bob planned the daring caper as a last payday to finance the gang's escape to South America. What better way for the Daltons to cap their outlaw careers than a bold stickup in broad daylight of two banks at once in the town where shiftless Lewis Dalton; his wife, Adeline Younger Dalton; and their plentiful brood of children had lived on two different occasions?

The scheme had been hatched near Tulsa in late September, and the gang had spent the last several days riding north. Now, on the outskirts of Coffeyville, they turned east along

The Condon Bank building, which the Daltons tried to rob, as it appears today.

a road leading into town that became Eighth Street. The Daltons donned disguises to keep from being recognized as they entered their old hometown. Each man carried at least two handguns, and each had a Winchester rifle in his saddle boot. Two separate couples, going the opposite direction, met the gang and thought nothing of them.

Bob's plan started going awry as soon as the gang hit town. Instead of reconnoitering Coffeyville, he had relied on his memory of how things used to be, but he quickly found things had changed since he had last been here over two years before. The hitching rail on Eighth Street near the rear of the Condon Bank, where the gang had planned to tie their horses, had been removed because of street construction. It may have seemed like a minor detail at the time, but it proved to be the Daltons' undoing.

Instead of tying their horses where they had planned, the gang rode to an alley a block and a half to the southwest and tethered their mounts to a metal pipe along a fence at the back of a lot. Then they started east on foot through the long alley, which came out on the town plaza 350 feet away, near the south-facing Condon Bank. Nobody paid much attention until they reached the end of the alley, where Alex McKenna was sweeping the sidewalk in front of his dry-goods business. As the outlaws started across Walnut Street toward the Condon, McKenna recognized one of the Daltons, despite their whiskery disguises. He watched Grat Dalton lead Broadwell and Power into the Condon while Bob and Emmett crossed Union Street toward the First National on the east side of the plaza.

When McKenna saw one of the bandits brandish a Winchester inside the Condon, he immediately gave the alarm. As word of the raid spread, the men of the town, who normally didn't carry guns on the streets, hurried to take up arms. At the Isham Brothers' and Boswell's hardware stores, both located on the east side of the plaza, clerks started handing out rifles and ammunition, and the freshly armed citizens took up strategic positions around the plaza.

Portraits of the men who defended Coffeyville on display at Dalton Defenders Museum.

Inside the Condon Bank, the robbers leveled their Winchesters at the employees, and Grat tossed a grain sack to cashier Charles Ball. Punctuating his demand with threats and curses, he told another employee, Charles Carpenter, to fill it with the contents of the cash drawers while Ball held it. After the men complied, Grat herded them into the vault, where he discovered three bags of silver dollars inside an open safe and ordered the coins dumped into the grain bag as well. Another large safe, bearing a sturdy combination lock, was firmly closed. Grat ordered Ball to open it, but the cashier coolly told the outlaw he couldn't because the safe was set on a time lock and wouldn't go off for another ten minutes. Believing the lie and completely unaware of the army of citizens forming outside, the gullible Grat said he would wait.

Meanwhile, Bob and Emmett Dalton burst into the First National and forced the employees and customers at gunpoint to gather into a small group in the front room. Bob called cashier Thomas Ayers by name and told him to put all the bank's money into a gunnysack that the Daltons produced. Showing some of the same gumption exhibited by cashier Ball at the Condon, Ayers took his time filling the sack by making several trips into the vault. After his last trip, Bob asked him if that was all, and the cashier replied that it was. Unlike his gullible brother, Bob decided to check for himself. He returned furious and carrying two more sacks of money containing $5,000 each. He dumped the contents into the grain sack, which now contained about $20,000.

Using the bank employees as shields, the Daltons started out the front door, but shots rang out when Ayers stepped outside. The Daltons ducked back into the bank and went out the back door, where they met a young man named Lucius Baldwin walking toward them with a pistol in his hand. When he continued walking closer after the Daltons told him to stop, Bob shot him dead.

With Emmett lugging the money and Bob wielding his Winchester, the brothers ran north to Eighth Street and started west, taking a circuitous route back to their horses. When they reached Union Street, shoemaker George Cubine was standing on the sidewalk near his shop with a rifle watching the front door of the First National. Bob shot him in the back and he fell dead. Another shoemaker, Charley

A photograph of dead Dalton gang members on display at Dalton Defenders Museum.

Brown, who was standing nearby, promptly grabbed Cubine's gun, and Bob shot him dead, too. After crossing the street, Bob also shot Thomas Ayers, who, after being shoved out the bank's door, had procured a rifle from Ishams' Hardware. He survived despite being hit squarely in the face.

The Daltons continued west past Walnut Street and turned south along a narrow passageway leading to the alley where they had tied their horses. Meanwhile, bullets were flying at a furious pace on the plaza as citizens showered the Condon Bank with approximately eighty shots. The three outlaws inside made a break for it, dashing across the plaza toward the alley through a hail of lead. Injured to varying degrees, they reached the alley about the same time Bob and Emmett emerged from the narrow passageway.

Later dubbed "Death Alley," the lane where the horses were tied became a shooting gallery for the marksmen at Ishams' Hardware and other strategically positioned citizens. Bob Dalton fell first. Grat slumped against a building but was able to rise and shoot Marshal Charles Connelly dead when the lawman appeared in the alley. Liveryman John Kloehr

The headstone of Bob Dalton, Grat Dalton, and Bill Power at Elmwood Cemetery in Coffeyville.

finished Grat with a rifle shot through the neck. Bill Power fell dead about ten feet west of Grat.

Only Broadwell and Emmett Dalton reached their horses. Broadwell rode away but fell dead from the saddle just outside town. Emmett was filled with lead when he turned his horse back down the alley to try to help his dying brother Bob. Amazingly, he survived to stand trial and go to prison.

Monument to the Dalton defenders in downtown Coffeyville

Dalton Defenders Museum at Coffeyville

After the four citizens who had met the outlaws riding into town learned of the raid, all swore they had seen six men. No one else in town saw more than five men, and Emmett Dalton himself said there were only five gang members at Coffeyville, but the four citizens' testimony has given rise to more than a century's worth of speculation about a mysterious "sixth rider."

Over the years, the Daltons have been romanticized in movies and song, but Coffeyville's Dalton Defenders Museum is rightly dedicated not to immortalizing outlaws, but to commemorating the brave men who risked and gave their lives protecting their town. The museum is open daily except for Easter, Thanksgiving, and Christmas. Hours are 9:00 A.M. to 5:00 P.M. March through October and 10:00 A.M. to 4 P.M. November through February. Admission is three dollars for adults. For more information, call the Coffeyville Chamber of Commerce at 620-251-2550.

16

Bill Doolin Wasn't Foolin':
The Southwest City Bank Robbery

When Bill Doolin and his Wild Bunch robbed the bank in Southwest City, Missouri, on May 10, 1894, almost one hundred shots rang out across Main Street in a shootout between the outlaws and the town's citizens. The wild exchange of lead threatened to turn the escapade into a reenactment of the fiasco at Coffeyville, Kansas, a year and a half earlier when four members of the Dalton gang and four citizens were killed and a fifth outlaw was seriously wounded during a holdup attempt. Unlike the outcome of the earlier venture, though, the outlaws got the best of the melee at Southwest City.

Doolin was born in Johnson County, Arkansas, in 1858, and grew up there. In 1881, he drifted west. For the next decade, he worked on ranches in Kansas and Oklahoma Territory and was considered a steady hand. His first brush with the law came around the Fourth of July of 1891 near Coffeyville when he and several other cowboys decided to celebrate the holiday by throwing a beer party. Kansas was a dry state at the time, and when local constables showed up to try to confiscate the refreshments, a shootout ensued, leaving two lawmen wounded. Soon afterwards, Doolin joined the Dalton gang.

However, for some reason, he missed the debacle at Coffeyville in October of 1892, which virtually wiped out the gang. One story says he sensed trouble and, feigning a thrown shoe on his horse, backed out of the robbery at the last minute. Another story claims Doolin was the mysterious "sixth rider" who, according to legend, held the gang's horses in an alley during the holdup attempt and managed to escape after the robbery went awry.

For whatever reason, Doolin came out of the Coffeyville disaster unscathed and emerged as leader of the gang. He formed the few remaining members, along with new recruits, into his own band called the Wild Bunch. Members of the gang included Bill Dalton, the last of the outlaw Dalton brothers, and other colorful characters like George "Bitter Creek" Newcomb, Bill "Tulsa Jack" Blake, Charlie "Black Face" Pierce, George "Red Buck" Weightman, Richard "Dynamite Dick" Clifton, Richard "Little Dick" West, and William "Little Bill" Raidler. During the next year and a half, the gang robbed several banks and trains throughout Kansas, Indian Territory, and Oklahoma Territory and was involved in a number of shootouts with law officers, including the infamous gunfight at Ingalls in Oklahoma Territory on September 1, 1893.

Slightly more than eight months later, on May 10, 1894, seven members of the gang rode into Southwest City, located in the extreme southwest corner of Missouri, at about 3:30 in the afternoon. The masked and heavily armed men rode in from the south and approached Main Street without making any demonstration until they got to the post office, where they dismounted and tied their horses. Punctuating their language with spectacular oaths, they told everyone on the street to "hunt holes." To give the command added force, they fired off a round of warning shots from their Winchesters.

The old bank building in Southwest City the Doolin gang held up as it appears today.

The outlaws then kept up a sporadic fusillade as three of them started for the nearby bank of A. F. Ault. Meanwhile, the other four took up lookout positions, two in a pool hall across the street from the post office and the remaining two in the lawn of a Dr. Nichols's residence near the bank. (Bailey C. Hanes's 1968 biography of Doolin identifies the three men who entered the bank as Doolin, Dalton, and Newcomb. Although Doolin probably did enter the bank, most recent authors agree that Dalton and Newcomb were not even present at Southwest City.)

The men inside the bank quickly got the drop on Mr. Ault and his assistant, a Mr. Snyder, while those outside continued firing at anyone who dared to show his head. Two of the men inside jumped onto the counter and crawled through the cashier's window, while the third guarded the bankers with his revolver, forcing them to put their hands over their heads and face the wall. The first two rifled through the cashier's drawer and ransacked the vault, filling a sack with all the money they could find, which came to about $3,700. In their haste, they overlooked another $5,000 in bank notes that was

Main Street of Southwest City, where the shootout with the Doolin gang occurred, as it looks today.

bound in several packages. After less than ten minutes inside the bank, the three robbers started back toward their horses, marching the two bankers in front of them as hostages.

Meanwhile, the alarm had been raised among citizens. Some of them had secured arms and started returning fire, while others still scurried about helter-skelter. Former state senator J. C. Seabourn and his brother Oscar were among the men on the street. Both were shot in nearly the same place above the right hip as they started to duck inside a hardware store. (One account of this incident says that a single shot fired from the blazing pistol of Little Dick West struck both brothers, passing through Oscar's lower body and lodging in Senator Seabourn's abdomen. This embellished version is contradicted, though, by contemporaneous newspaper reports, which suggest the two men were struck by separate bullets and that Oscar was the one who had the bullet lodged in him.) J. C. Seabourn died of his wound four days later; his brother eventually recovered. Another citizen, M. V. Hembree, received a ball in the ankle that almost severed his leg, as he sought shelter inside Barker's Saloon. One witness said nearly one hundred shots were fired on Main Street during the robbery and that it "sounded like war times."

When the gang reached their horses, they released the hostages, then commenced firing in every direction and "tore down the street toward the Territory border at breakneck speed." As they turned south on Broadway, they encountered a determined resistance from several townspeople, including Deputy U. S. Marshal Simpson Melton and City Marshal Carlyle, who had gathered on both sides of the road to give them "a warm reception." In the exchange of shots, at least two of the gang were wounded, including Doolin, who was peppered with buckshot on the side of his head but managed to stay in the saddle. One of the gang's horses was also hit, and Melton received a flesh wound in the leg. Continuing their retreat, the outlaws came to the residence of a man named J. D. Powell. He opened fire on them as they rode by, wounding another of their horses. Two other citizens,

Charles Franks and Dick Prather, also "gave them a dose" as the outlaws passed the local Baptist church.

On the outskirts of Southwest City, the gang waylaid two citizens driving wagons and cut a horse from each rig to replace the mounts that had been injured while running the gauntlet of Broadway Street. One of the new animals, though, wasn't fast enough to suit the outlaws; so, they turned it loose and stole another from a nearby farmhouse. (Although Doolin's favorite horse, Old Dick, was among those wounded, it was not disabled enough to abandon. Doolin finally sold the animal, however, to a doctor in Ingalls, because its injury had left it no longer valuable as a saddle horse.)

A few miles outside town, the outlaws stopped another team driven by Jim Van Hooser, who was escorting his sister, a Mrs. Sharpe, from his home in Indian Territory to her home in Siloam Springs, Arkansas. Van Hooser balked when the gang first demanded one of his horses, but they raised their Winchesters and "soon convinced him that they wanted the horse badly."

Several hours after the bank robbery, a posse from Southwest City finally organized and started in pursuit of the bandits, tracking them in a southwesterly direction into Indian Territory, also known as the Indian Nation or simply the Nation. The outlaws stopped for supper that evening roughly twelve or fourteen miles below Southwest City, where they dressed their wounds. The woman who prepared the meal for them said later that six of the seven gang members were injured. The posse, however, failed to catch up with the outlaws and finally lost track of them some distance below Grand River. About a week later, one newspaper reported that the robbers had not been heard from, and "the probabilities are they never will be."

Various parties were suspected of participating in the Southwest City bank holdup, and a reward of $1,700 was offered for the capture of the robbers. One newspaper speculated in the immediate aftermath of the caper that it had no doubt been carried out by "the Starr and Dalton

gang, which for years has had a rendezvous in the rough hills
not more than thirty or forty miles southwest of Southwest
City." Mrs. Sharpe claimed to have recognized several men
whom she knew to be associated with the Henry Starr gang
as being among the seven who had waylaid her and her
brother outside Southwest City on the day of the robbery. At
least two of the men she named, Alf Chaney and Dr. Charles
Wynn, had been strongly implicated in helping Starr rob the
Bentonville Bank on June 5, 1893. However, at the time of
the Southwest City Bank holdup, Alf Chaney was already in
jail for his part in the Starr gang's May 1893 train robbery
at Pryor Creek in Indian Territory, a circumstance that casts
doubt on Mrs. Sharpe's entire testimony.

On the other hand, evidence exists to suggest that Dr.
Wynn, a known associate and abettor of outlaws, was, indeed,
involved in the Southwest City robbery. Hanes says in his
biography that the Doolin gang spent the night at Wynn's
home at Fairland, Indian Territory, on the evening before
the Southwest City holdup, that the doctor cased the town
for the outlaws before they entered it, and that they returned
to his home after the escapade to have their wounds treated.
Although contemporaneous newspaper reports cast doubt
on the latter assertion (because they say the robbers were
trailed in a southwesterly direction, while Fairland lies
considerably northwest of Southwest City), Wynn was, in
fact, widely suspected of having aided in the robbery. He
and a man named Sparks were quickly arrested, but Sparks
was soon discharged for lack of evidence. Wynn was held in
jail until the next term of court, at which time he, too, was
released when the grand jury failed to bring an indictment
against him. A third man, James Condry, was later arrested in
connection with the robbery and indicted, but his case was
nol-prossed because of lack of evidence.

Other men identified by Mrs. Sharpe as being among the
ones who stole the horse from her brother outside Southwest
City or who were otherwise suspected of participating in
the robbery included Henry Roberts, Bill Cornett, Tom

Crather, and Bill Doolin. Although most of these men were apparently not involved in the robbery, they were all considered desperate characters, and Crather was shortly afterwards killed on the Grand River in Indian Territory by a posse of fifty men sent out in response to the crime.

Of the suspects identified in the days immediately following the Southwest City Bank robbery, apparently only Doolin was an active participant. In reference to the robbery, the 1897 *Illustrated History of McDonald County* concluded, "In the course of time, it was demonstrated to the satisfaction of most of the people of the town that the raid had been made by Bill Doolin and his gang." Most modern sources suggest that the other members of the gang who made the jaunt to Southwest City were Blake, Clifton, Pierce, Raidler, Weightman, and West.

The Wild Bunch continued to rob and raid throughout Kansas and Oklahoma Territory during the next year and a half. Then, in January of 1896, legendary U. S. marshal Bill Tilghman finally caught up with Bill Doolin in Eureka Springs, Arkansas. The outlaw had gone there to seek treatment for a rheumatic leg he had developed as a result of being shot in the foot during a train robbery near Cimarron, Kansas, in June of 1893. Tilghman found Doolin in a bathhouse, where he had registered under the alias of Tom Wilson, and arrested him without incident. The hombre was taken back to Guthrie in Oklahoma Territory and placed in jail, but less than six months later, he and about ten other prisoners escaped. In late August of 1896, a month and a half after the jail break, Doolin was killed in a shootout with Deputy U. S. Marshal Heck Thomas near Lawson, Oklahoma.

One hundred and some-odd years later, Bill Doolin, like so many outlaws of his era, has become an almost mythical figure, and he has even been romanticized in movies and song. Randolph Scott, for example, played Bill Doolin in the 1949 release *The Doolins of Oklahoma*, and the Eagles' *Desperado* album, released in the early 1970s, was inspired by the story

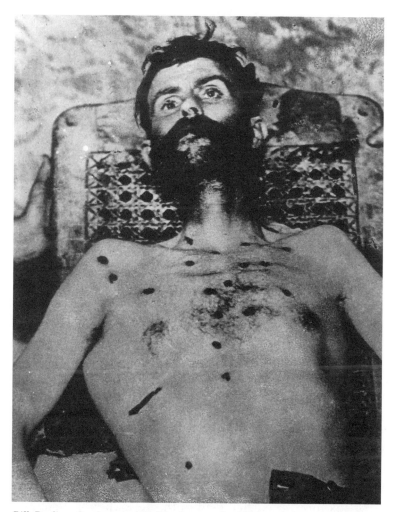

Bill Doolin after he was killed by lawmen in 1896 near Lawson, Oklahoma Territory. (Courtesy University of Oklahoma, Western History Collections)

of the Doolin and Dalton gangs. The people of Southwest City no doubt would have sung a different song in 1894. To them, there was nothing romantic about Bill Doolin and his notorious Wild Bunch.

17

House of Sport, House of Murder

The Galena (Kansas) Mining Museum, the local Sonic Drive-In, and a couple of other businesses sit near where once stood the Staffelbach residence, a noted "house of ill-fame" during Galena's rip-roaring mining days. One hundred and twelve years later, motorists drive past the area on West Seventh Street in Galena every day never imagining that it was once the scene of the town's most notorious crime.

Between ten and eleven o'clock on the night of June 19, 1897, thirty-two-year-old Frank Galbraith and his drinking buddy, Jesse Jacobs, called at the Staffelbach home on the west edge of Galena. Galbraith asked to see a girl named Emma Chapman, but the young woman sent word that she was otherwise "engaged" and suggested he return later.

Galbraith and Jacobs walked back to downtown Galena to "continu[e] the process of imbibing." City Marshal Parker spotted the pair on the streets and suggested to Galbraith that he ought to quit drinking. Galbraith had a reputation about town as a friendly drunk who was "never bothersome" and would only "stagger around in people's way." However, Marshal Parker had been forced to toss him in jail for public intoxication two or three times since Galbraith had moved to the area from neighboring Fort Scott six months earlier. Galbraith, nevertheless, declined the marshal's invitation to abstain.

Around two o'clock in the morning, Galbraith suggested to Jacobs that they take another drink and then "go back to see the girls." Jacobs, though, was ready to call it a night. He said he'd had enough to drink and didn't feel like going back to the Staffelbach house. As Jacobs started away, Galbraith vowed to go back with or without him.

Galbraith returned to the Staffelbach house alone around

The area where the Staffelbach home sat as it appears today.

3:00 A.M., and sixty-five-year-old Nancy Staffelbach, madam of the premises and matriarch of the Staffelbach family, met him at the door, while several other residents of the home stood in the background. When Galbraith again asked to see Emma Chapman, the old woman told him Emma didn't want to see him. Galbraith remonstrated that he had a note from the girl stating otherwise and that he intended to go in and find out for himself whether Emma wanted to see him. Reaching for a nearby corn knife, Old Lady Staffelbach flew at Galbraith in a rage. "Let me at him!" she shouted as she brandished the weapon. "I'll kill him with this corn knife. I'll cut off his damn head."

Aroused by the commotion, Ed and George Staffelbach, Nancy's sons, and Charles Wilson, her "pretended husband," sprang to her aid. Mrs. Staffelbach's first husband had died a few years earlier, and she had recently taken up with Wilson, although the couple apparently had never legally married. Wilson, who was just back from a brief stay in the Cherokee County jail at Columbus, and the Staffelbach boys went after Galbraith with pistols and knives, pursuing him toward Seventh Street, the main road running west out of Galena.

Ed Staffelbach fired one shot at Galbraith, and he or one of the other pursuers fired a second time before the fleeing man fell to his hands and knees near a trash dump. When he tried to rise, a third shot was fired. Galbraith threw up his hand to cover his head and tried to get up again.

Ed Staffelbach stood over the fallen man flourishing a pocketknife as Anna McCombs, Ed's common-law wife, and Cora Staffelbach, George's wife, rushed up, having trailed the men from the house. Anna grabbed Ed's arm. "Don't!" she yelled. "You'll kill him."

With Anna hanging on his arm, Ed Staffelbach slashed the right side of Galbraith's face and neck. Blood spurted on Staffelbach's shirt and pants, as Galbraith's lifeless body slumped back to the ground.

"Now you have killed him," Anna wailed.

George Staffelbach, standing next to Cora, asked, "Why the hell don't Annie leave Ed alone?"

After the murder, Ed Staffelbach told Annie not to say a word about what had happened or he would kill her. Then the men ordered the women back to the house and began rifling through the dead man's pockets. The two women ambled a short distance toward the house before stopping to look back. Soon they heard the splash of Galbraith's body as the three men dropped the corpse into a nearby, abandoned mining shaft that was half filled with water.

The women returned to the house, and when the Staffelbach boys showed up a few minutes later, their mother gave Ed a change of clothes and fixed chili for the whole group. Charles Wilson came home sometime after daylight carrying the hat Galbraith had been wearing the night before and started cleaning it with soap and water.

A month later, on the morning of July 19, 1897, a stranger was tramping his way into Galena along West Seventh Street when he paused to gaze into the old abandoned shaft that set just north of the road about a quarter mile from Main Street. He was shocked to see a man's body about thirty feet down, floating on top of the water. The passerby rushed to Main

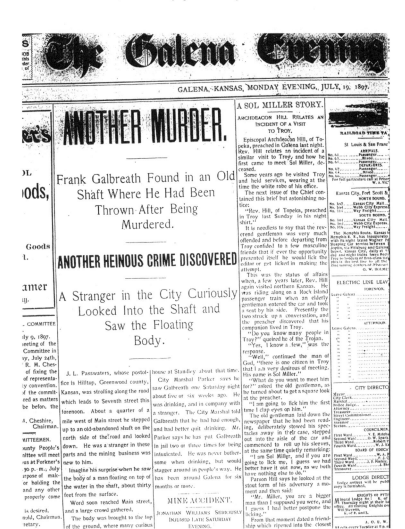

Galena newspaper headline detailing the murder of Frank Galbraith

Street with the news, and a curious crowd quickly gathered at the shaft. The badly decomposed body was hauled to the surface and identified as Galbraith by letters found in a coat pocket. The man had obviously been murdered, because he had a bullet hole in his left side above the hip, another behind his left ear, his throat slashed, and cuts on his face.

Authorities held an inquest, at which Marshal Parker and others testified they had last seen Galbraith on a night about five weeks earlier in the company of an unknown man. Cherokee County deputy sheriff Charles Rains set out to locate the stranger and sent Constable Lafe Roe and Deputy Constable L. M. Radley to hunt down anyone who might remember hearing shots fired in the vicinity of the abandoned mineshaft near the suspected time of Galbraith's murder. Rains located Jesse Jacobs, who told the lawmen of Galbraith's determination to visit the Staffelbach house on the fateful night. Meanwhile, Rains's deputies inquired of numerous miners and finally located one who told them he had heard three shots near the Staffelbach home, which was also near the abandoned shaft, on approximately the night in question.

This confluence of circumstances cast immediate suspicion on the Staffelbachs. Upon inquiry, officers learned that Anna McCombs, Cora Staffelbach, and two other former residents of the Staffelbach home had moved to nearby Joplin since the night of the murder. A party of lawmen went to Joplin on the evening of July 27 to interrogate the group. They found the sporting women at a "free and easy" in Joplin, and Deputy Rains extracted a confession from Anna McCombs and Cora Staffelbach, eyewitnesses to the murder. The pair told Rains that Ed Staffelbach had done most of the work but that Old Lady Staffelbach, her son George, and Charles Wilson were also involved in the crime.

The two women were not charged in the murder but were held as witnesses and taken back to Galena by train the same night. Upon their return, the officers immediately set about rounding up the principals in the crime. They arrested Nancy Staffelbach at her home and found Ed Staffelbach on Main Street. Locating George Staffelbach proved to be no problem, as he was already a guest of the county jail in Columbus for breaking into a boxcar a couple of weeks earlier. Charles Wilson was taken into custody the next day. Ed and George Staffelbach were charged with first-degree murder, while their mother and Wilson were charged with second-degree murder.

The Staffelbachs had a history of run-ins with the law dating back at least to July of 1878 when Johnny Staffelbach, brother of Ed and George, went on the warpath in the Joplin neighborhood where the family lived at the time, breaking furniture and threatening to kill "an imaginary enemy." The young man's father, Michel Staffelbach, fearful that his "insane son" would hurt himself or others, had to enlist the help of neighbors to subdue the twenty-one-year-old Johnny. The *Joplin Daily Herald* reported at the time that young Staffelbach had often created disturbances on the streets in the past during similar "crazy spells."

After their arrest for the murder of Galbraith, the Staffelbachs were compared in newspaper headlines to the Bloody Benders (see chapter 6) and were denounced as longstanding troublemakers. The *Joplin Globe* reported, "The Staffelbach gang formerly resided in this city, and much deviltry is charged up against them during their residence here." The *Joplin News* added, "The Staffelbach family has been a disgrace to the human race in general and the inhabitants of Joplin and vicinity in particular for many years."

The family was mentioned specifically in connection with at least two unsolved murders. By mid 1895, Michel Staffelbach, a candy maker from Switzerland, had either died or deserted the family "because of their mean, thieving disposition," and Old Lady Staffelbach started consorting with an old, married man named Rosenbaugh. On Christmas Day of 1895, Rosenbaugh started for the old woman's shack at 1101 Ivy Street (now Connor) in Joplin with a large sum of money on his person and was never heard from again. Foul play was immediately suspected, but the Staffelbachs were not implicated at the time despite the fact they left for Galena soon afterwards. Only in retrospect, after the Galbraith murder came to light, was the family suspected of killing Rosenbaugh.

In February of 1897, the body of a man named Matt McGuirk was found in an abandoned mineshaft not far from where the Staffelbachs lived in Galena. McGuirk had been bashed in the head, fracturing his skull in several places, before being dropped into the shaft. When the Staffelbachs were arrested for the Galbraith murder, the similar circumstances between it and the McGuirk case caused suspicion to fall on the Staffelbachs in regard to the earlier murder as well.

Then, at the Staffelbachs' trial for Galbraith's murder, held in September of 1897 at Columbus, Cora Staffelbach implicated Ed and another brother, Mike Staffelbach, in two more grisly murders. She said that in January of 1896, just after the family had moved from Joplin to Galena, Ed and Mike Staffelbach brought two new girls to the house and deposited them there with an understanding that they should reserve their affections for the Staffelbach men. One night shortly afterwards, though, Mike came home and found one of the girls sitting in the lap of a gentleman caller. He flew into a jealous rage, ordered the man off the premises, and started beating the girl. When the other girl came to her friend's aid, Ed appeared on the scene and started beating the second girl for interfering. Mike killed the first girl with pistol blows to the head, and Ed choked and beat the life out of the second girl with his bare hands. Both bodies were tossed in a mineshaft.

After Cora Staffelbach's testimony, a search was made of the shaft where she said the bodies were dumped. A few scraps of women's clothing were found but no bodies or other evidence was discovered. The Staffelbachs were not charged in this or any of the other crimes in which they were implicated after their arrest for Galbraith's murder.

The Galbraith case was enough. All four defendants were convicted of murder. George Staffelbach was sentenced to death with the term later commuted to life in prison. His brother Ed, after a hearing to determine his sanity, was given the same treatment. Their mother, Nancy Staffelbach, drew a sentence of twenty-one years, and Charles Wilson received twenty-five years in prison. During the same term of court, Mike Staffelbach, who was already in the county jail on a charge of larceny at the time of Galbraith's murder, was convicted of the charge and given seven years in prison.

In 1909, Nancy Staffelbach died of pneumonia in the Kansas state penitentiary at the age of seventy-seven. At the time she died, one of the two sons who had been convicted with her in the Galbraith case had already died in prison, and the other one was still serving his life term. Mike had completed his seven-year term at Lansing and had taken up residence at the Missouri state prison in Jefferson City as punishment for another crime.

Today no sign of the shaft where Galbraith's body was found remains, and the Staffelbach shanty has long ago been torn down. If you walk out behind the businesses that line the north side of West Seventh Street, though, and gaze out across the landscape left desolate by mining, you can almost imagine the ghosts of Galena's most infamous criminals still haunting the place.

18

Cora Hubbard and
the Pineville Bank Robbery

On August 21, 1897, the day twenty-seven-year-old Cora Hubbard was arrested for robbing the McDonald County Bank in Pineville, Missouri, she stunned observers with her unrepentant attitude. Cora told the *Daily Herald* in nearby Joplin that she was "not a damn bit" afraid during the robbery and suggested her only regret was that she and her accomplices hadn't "held up the whole damn town."

Cora and her sidekicks had hatched the bank robbery scheme a month earlier on a farm in Indian Territory (present-day Oklahoma) near Nowata, where Cora had taken up residence with her new husband, Bud Parker. She had married Parker around July 1 after divorcing her previous husband just two months earlier. Twenty-three-year-old John Sheets was working on Parker's farm as a hired hand, and thirty-one-year-old Whit Tennyson drifted in about the time Parker brought home his new bride. Two of Cora's brothers, Al and William "Bill" Hubbard, were also living in the area at least part time.

Tennyson claimed to be experienced in the "work" of bank robbery, and he soon had the destitute bunch at the farm "in the notion of helping him out" on his next caper. The gang picked the McDonald County Bank at Pineville because Bill Hubbard had lived there briefly and knew the town's layout. He sketched a diagram of the place, and Parker, Sheets, Tennyson, and Al Hubbard were supposed to carry out the scheme. However, when it came time, Al Hubbard and Bud Parker decided against the escapade. In anger at her new husband, Cora rode off toward Kansas with Sheets and Tennyson, declaring she would not live with "a damn coward."

The downsized gang stopped in Coffeyville, Kansas, long

Cora Hubbard poses for the camera after her arrest for robbing the Pineville bank.
(Courtesy McDonald County Library)

enough for Sheets to buy a Winchester and ammunition
and then continued to Cora's hometown of Weir City,
Kansas, where her father, Sam Hubbard, had worked in the
coalmines. The old man was startled to see his daughter with
her hair cut short, wearing men's clothes, and accompanied

by Sheets, a young desperado Sam had never seen before. As he later explained, he couldn't bring himself to turn his daughter away, since she was "a motherless girl." After lolling around Weir for a few days and procuring more ammunition, the unlikely trio started for Pineville in the southwest corner of Missouri over sixty miles away.

They arrived in the Pineville area on August 16, 1897, and spent the night just outside town. The next morning, Sheets and Tennyson went into town to check the place out one last time before putting their daring design into action. Finding nothing to make them reconsider their plan, they returned to camp to get Cora.

All three rode back into town and stopped at a barn located on a private residence about a block from the bank. Cora held the gang's horses there while Sheets and Tennyson marched off toward the bank. When the landowner's son appeared at the barn door, Cora pointed her gun and told the lad to stand still. He did "just as he was told," but to Cora he appeared a bit nervous. "It's no use to get excited at a time like this," she remarked calmly.

Sheets and Tennyson, meanwhile, sneaked around the corner of the bank and pointed their weapons at the three men sitting out front—A. V. Manning, president of the bank; John W. Shields, cashier; and Marcus N. LaMance, county treasurer. "We're here for the money and we want it damn quick," one of the outlaws announced as they ordered the two bank officers inside.

With his partner outside guarding LaMance, Sheets herded the two men into the bank, poking them with his rifle. Two ladies in a buggy promptly drove up to the hitch stand in front of the bank, and Tennyson greeted them with a threatening wave of his weapon. "Just sit still and you shan't be hurt," he told them.

Inside the bank, Shields turned to protest, but Sheets knocked him to the floor with his rifle and sent him scrambling on all fours toward the vault. Lacing his demands with profanity, Sheets told Manning to hold a sack and ordered Shields to fill it with money. Shields quickly crammed in all the coins and currency he could lay his hands on, a total of $589.23.

With the cash in hand, Sheets forced Shields and Manning out of the bank. He and Tennyson herded the two bank officials through the street at "a lively trot" along the same route the outlaws had come, using the bankers as a shield to keep bystanders from shooting. Along the way, Tennyson relieved Manning of his $15 silver watch. When the group reached the barn, Sheets, Tennyson, and Cora mounted their horses and rode out of town to the northeast, the same way they had come in. One of the bandits fired a shot into the air to punctuate their escape as they galloped away.

A mile down the road, the robbers met Floyd Shields, the banker's eleven-year-old son. The boy was riding a bay mare named Birdie, and Tennyson took the animal in exchange for his own. In Pineville, a posse quickly formed and trailed the bandits out of town. When the gang circled Pineville and changed directions, one of the deputies came back to town to report that the brigands were headed to Indian Territory, and news of the robbery and a description of the outlaws were quickly wired to Noel, five miles to the southwest. The bandit who had remained at the stable was identified as "a small young man or boy, part Indian."

Late in the afternoon, two miles south of Noel, the pursuers from Pineville got beyond the outlaws and joined another posse from Noel at the crossing of Butler Creek to lie in wait. When the fugitives rode down a gully toward the stream as anticipated, the six deputies opened fire. Tennyson and Sheets were filled with buckshot, Sheets's horse was badly wounded, and Cora's revolver was shot out of her hand. The gang managed to return fire, wounding one of the deputies, but Birdie, the horse Tennyson was riding, bolted away, separating him from his partners. In the meantime, Cora and Sheets turned their horses around and escaped back up the ravine through heavy timber before Sheets's horse collapsed and died from its wounds.

The deputies turned their attention to Tennyson. They found Birdie not far from the scene with her saddle still on but her bridle missing. At midmorning the next day, August 18, word reached Southwest City, in the extreme southwest corner of Missouri, that a man who fit the description of one of the robbers had eaten breakfast earlier that morning six miles to the west in Indian Territory and paid for it in pennies. This seemed to confirm that he was one of the robbers, because many one-cent pieces had been stolen from the bank. A posse headed by Joe Yeargain of Southwest City set out after the fugitive. That evening at an isolated cabin twenty miles inside the Territory, the group found a wounded Tennyson in possession of a bridle, a .45 Winchester, a .45 revolver, and $121.50 that had been taken in the robbery. He was captured without struggle and brought back to Southwest City, on to Pineville the next day, and then to nearby Neosho, where he was housed in the Newton County jail.

Tennyson identified his partners, and when word got out that one of them was a woman, the news caused a sensation. The headline of one area newspaper called Cora Hubbard the "Second Belle Starr," referring to the famous female "outlaw" in Indian Territory who was shot to death by an unknown person in 1889. Another headline read, "Female Bandit Rivals the Daring Deeds of Belle Starr and Kate Bender," the latter being the leading spirit of a murderous family that killed eight people in Kansas in the early 1870s. When authorities learned from Tennyson that Hubbard and Sheets were from Weir City, a posse headed by Yeargain and Shields set out for the outlaws' hometown.

Meanwhile, near the scene of the shootout in southwest Missouri, Cora had dismounted a man at gunpoint to get a new horse for Sheets, and the two rode west toward Kansas. They didn't halt until they reached Parsons seventy miles away. From there, Cora boarded a train back to Weir City on August 21. Sheets promised to follow in a day or two, and from Weir, the duo planned to escape to Iowa.

Cora had barely arrived at her father's home in Weir when

the posse hit town. They enlisted the help of City Marshal Jim Hatton, who scouted the Hubbard residence at the edge of town under the pretext of borrowing Sam Hubbard's tar kettle. The marshal saw that Cora was there and went back to the posse to report his findings. As the posse men were heading to the Hubbard residence to take Cora into custody, they met Bill Hubbard on the way and promptly arrested him for his part in the robbery. After taking him to jail, they returned to the Hubbard residence. One of the deputies knocked on the door with the muzzle of his rifle. When Cora opened the door, the deputy pointed his Winchester and told her to put up her hands. She obeyed with no sign of fear but rather, according to one report, "like a child at play putting up its hands before a toy pistol."

Now wearing a calico dress, Cora was hurried off to the city jail barefooted. Later the same day, she and her brother were escorted by train to Missouri, and during a stopover at a Joplin hotel, Joe Yeargain purchased some shoes and stockings for her. Cora put them on in front of a newspaperman "without any special display of modesty on her part." It was to this reporter that she boasted that her only regret was that she and her cohorts hadn't robbed the whole town.

On the evening of August 24, Marshal Hatton grew suspicious that some of the money taken in the bank robbery might be concealed at the Hubbard residence, and he and a deputy went back to search the premises. They unearthed $25 buried in a hill of peppers. The next day they came back and dug up another $166 buried in a hill of potatoes. At the residence, they also found the men's clothing Cora had worn during the holdup and a Colt .45 revolver with the name "Bob Dalton" etched on the handle and seven notches carved near the trigger guard. Cora had often claimed around Weir that she had been with the Dalton gang in earlier years and that she had Bob Dalton's gun. The discovery seemed to confirm what had previously been passed off as "idle boast," and the notches were presumed to represent the number of men killed with the Colt.

Marshal Hatton telegraphed Pineville concerning his

Cora Hubbard, Whit Tennyson, and John Sheets after their arrest for the Pineville bank robbery. (Courtesy McDonald County Library)

discoveries, and Shields and the McDonald County sheriff came to Weir on the morning of August 26. The officers had assembled at the Hubbard residence to grill Old Man Hubbard when John Sheets drove up unaware and was immediately arrested. Another $91 taken during the Pineville robbery and a .45 caliber six-shooter were found in the buggy. In addition to Sheets, Sam Hubbard was also arrested and hauled back to Missouri because of his grudging cooperation with officers in their search for the loot.

However, he and his son Bill were both released at Pineville on August 28, the same day the three bank robbers had their preliminary hearing. Cora Hubbard posed for a photograph dressed in the clothing she had donned during the holdup, and then she and her two sidekicks were bound over for trial and returned to the Newton County jail in Neosho. They were found guilty of bank robbery in January of 1898 and sentenced to the state penitentiary at Jefferson City—Cora and Sheets for twelve years each and Tennyson for ten. The Missouri governor commuted Cora's sentence the day after Christmas of 1904, and she was released on New Year's Day of 1905. During her imprisonment, the

McDonald County Court indictment of Cora Hubbard, Whit Tennyson, and John Sheets. (Courtesy McDonald County Library)

one-time bank robber had let her hair grow out but had apparently done little else to enhance her feminine allure in the eyes of the reporter who described her at the time of her release as "short in stature with . . . black eyes and a greasy dark complexion."

19

Henry Starr's Bentonville
and Harrison Bank Robberies

Henry Starr, a nephew by marriage of the so-called "Bandit Queen" Belle Starr, was a lad of just fourteen when he first ran afoul of the law in his native Indian Territory (Oklahoma) in 1888. Brought before a judge at Muskogee on a charge of peddling whiskey, he paid the fine and went back home to Nowata but soon graduated to more serious offenses like horse thievery. By the time he was nineteen, young Starr had robbed a train depot at Nowata; killed a deputy U. S. marshal sent out to apprehend him; held up a bank at Caney, Kansas; and pulled off a train robbery at Pryor Creek, Indian Territory.

Just a month after the Pryor Creek caper, Starr and his gang camped fifteen miles outside Bentonville, Arkansas, on the early morning of June 5, 1893, with plans to rob the People's Bank of Bentonville. Starr had cased the town the day before and rented a buggy in which to transport the gang's weapons across the farming district between the camp and the town so as not to arouse suspicion. Starr and Frank Cheney rode in the buggy, leading their horses, as the gang started toward Bentonville in the late morning. The other four gang members; Link Cumplin, Happy Jack, Hank Watt, and Kid Wilson; followed by twos about a mile apart. They closed up as they neared the town, and the gang approached the courthouse square together about 2:30 in the afternoon.

Starr and Cheney drove around the square and parked the buggy in an alley behind the office of the *Bentonville Sun*. The others followed and dismounted. While Happy Jack held the horses, the rest of the gang grabbed their rifles from beneath a blanket in the back of the buggy and rapidly walked a half block north to the bank. Watt took up a position covering the escape route back to the horses, Cumplin stood guard at the bank door, and Starr, Cheney, and Wilson hurried inside. Wielding their rifles, they forced the bank's president, A. W. Dinsmore; vice president, I. R. Hull; cashier, J. H. McAndrew; assistant cashier, George Jackson; and two customers against the wall and ordered them to keep their "thumbs up and stand ready."

Starr guarded the hostages as Cheney and Wilson set to work relieving the bank of all the cash they could find. Wilson leaped behind the counter and started going through the cashiers' drawers while Cheney entered the vault.

Meanwhile, some of the townspeople realized a bank robbery was in process and quickly spread the word. Citizens armed themselves with shotguns and rifles and opened fire on Watt and Cumplin outside the bank. A young boy ran to the courthouse to alert Sheriff Pierce Galbraith, who grabbed his rifle and raced toward the scene. Spotting the outlaws' horses in the alley, he opened fire on the man guarding them. Happy Jack hopped from foot to foot trying to dodge the bullets but managed to keep hold of the horses.

Inside the bank, Cheney and Wilson crammed all the money into two sacks, one containing $11,000 in gold and currency and the other $900 in silver, within five minutes. However, it took long enough that a full-fledged gun battle was now raging on the street outside. Starr grabbed the sack of gold and currency and handed the bag of silver to assistant cashier Jackson, freeing Cheney and Wilson to handle their Winchesters. Starr and his sidekicks herded the hostages out the door, meaning to use them as shields. The hail of bullets from the citizens' weapons that met them as they stepped outside prompted most of the captives to make a run for it, and they escaped before the outlaws could react. The robbers still had Jackson, but his presence scarcely deterred the barrage of gunfire. The cashier was wounded in two places as they marched him down Main Street, but a brave young woman named Maggie Wood who worked for the *Bentonville Sun* rescued him by reaching out and pulling him inside the newspaper office, bag of silver and all, as the group tramped by.

The gang paid little attention to the lost silver. With the guns of the citizens still blazing, there were more pressing

matters to attend to. The outlaws returned fire as they made
their way to their horses, wounding two citizens, Taylor Stone
and Tom Baker. The robbers were shot up as well, with Link
Cumplin wounded so badly that he couldn't use his rifle and
needed help mounting his horse.

The gang galloped out of town to the west, spurred on
by a final torrent of lead from the citizens' guns. Sheriff

Henry Starr circa 1915. (Courtesy Research Division of the Oklahoma
Historical Society)

Galbraith hastily organized a posse and gave chase. About twelve miles west of Bentonville, the lawmen intercepted the gang in the midst of robbing stores at the village of Decatur, and a running fight ensued. Three of the posse's horses were shot, but no one was injured. Shortly afterwards, with the approach of darkness, the sheriff and his deputies finally called off the pursuit and went back to Bentonville to check on their friends who had been injured.

Starr's gang rode all night and reached Cheney's farm near Wagoner, Indian Territory, about 3:00 P.M. the next day. Starr hid out for awhile and then made his way to Colorado, where he was recognized, arrested, and brought back in August of 1893 to Fort Smith, Arkansas, for trial. He was convicted of robbing the Nowata depot and the Pryor Creek train and of killing Deputy Marshal Floyd Wilson. He was sentenced to hang by Judge Isaac Parker, the "hanging judge," for the latter crime but was granted a new trial on appeal, and shortly afterwards, Parker lost control of Indian Territory in a jurisdictional realignment. Wanting to dispose of the pending cases promptly after the reorganization, the government struck a deal with Starr that called for him to serve a total of fifteen years for the three convictions.

Starr became a model prisoner, had his sentence commuted by Pres. Theodore Roosevelt, and was released on January 16, 1903. Starr got married, had a baby boy whom he named after Roosevelt, and tried to go straight for a while. In 1907, though, when Arkansas authorities began trying to extradite him for the Bentonville job, he went on the lam rather than face the charge. He pulled off a string of bank robberies in Oklahoma and Kansas in the fall of 1907 and early 1908 and then moved west into Colorado, New Mexico, and Arizona. He was arrested in 1909 for robbing a bank at Amity, Colorado, and sentenced to serve from seven to twenty-five years in the Colorado penitentiary.

Again, though, he became an exemplary prisoner and was paroled in 1913 under the condition that he report regularly and not leave the state of Colorado. He took a job at a restaurant but got involved with a married woman, and they ran away together to Arizona, making him a fugitive once again. During the fall of 1914 and the winter of 1915, he pulled off another string of robberies in Oklahoma and was finally wounded and captured while holding up a bank at Stroud on March 15, 1915. He pled guilty to the Stroud bank robbery and was sent to the Oklahoma penitentiary for twenty-five years.

As usual, he was soon able to convince prison authorities that he had reformed, and he was granted parole on March 15, 1919, partly because the wounds he suffered at Stroud had left him "permanently crippled" and he was no longer thought to be a danger to society. Starr made at least three movies, silent Westerns in which he portrayed himself, and again appeared to be trying to go straight. He got married again, and in early February of 1921, he visited his son, who was now a senior in high school, at Muskogee, Oklahoma.

Just two weeks later, however, on the morning of February 18, Starr and three sidekicks roared into Harrison, Arkansas, in a high-powered touring car and circled the town cutting down communication wires. They proceeded to the People's National Bank and parked on the street outside the building. The driver stayed in the car while Starr and the other two robbers walked boldly into the bank and presented their weapons. Starr's two accomplices stood guard near the front of the bank as he went behind the tellers' cage and gathered up about $6,000 in currency from the tills. Stuffing the money into his pockets, he turned to a cashier, G. C. Hoffman, and ordered him to open the safe, where the bulk of the currency was kept.

About this time, a customer entered the bank, momentarily diverting the attention of the two robbers who were standing guard. W. J. Meyers, a stockholder and former president of the bank, quickly darted inside a vault, near where he had been standing, that was used for storing bank papers and financial records. Retrieving a Winchester from a rack at the rear of the vault that was kept there for just such an emergency, Meyers returned to the entrance and fired one

The fast action of former bank president W. J. Meyers halted Starr in his tracks.
(Courtesy Boone County Heritage Museum and the *Ozarks Mountaineer*)

shot at Starr as the outlaw was stooped beside Hoffman monitoring his opening of the safe.

The bullet struck Starr in the lower side, passed through his spinal column, and lodged in his back. As he fell to the floor partially paralyzed, his accomplices threatened to open fire on the hostages, but Starr yelled that he was "done for." He told his partners to make their escape, and the two bandits ran out of the bank to the awaiting getaway car. Toting the same gun with which he had shot Starr, the sixty-year-old Meyers gave chase and fired seven shots but did little damage except to puncture a rear tire in the fleeing vehicle. The bandits returned fire but didn't hit Meyers.

The crooks roared south out of town, with a hastily formed posse under Sheriff J. Sibley Johnson in pursuit. Two miles outside Harrison, the punctured tire forced the bandits to halt and abandon the vehicle, which they set fire to before fleeing on foot into nearby woods. The posse made a thorough search of the area but turned up no sign of the robbers, and the sheriff and his deputies returned to Harrison late that night.

Meanwhile, Henry Starr was taken to the county jail, where a physician removed the bullet from his body, but he was not expected to recover. Adhering to the thieves' code of honor, Starr positively refused to identify the other men who had participated in the Harrison robbery with him. He announced with some pride to his attending physician, "I have robbed more banks than any man in the United States."

"But it doesn't pay," he added, and he expressed remorse for the course his life had taken. Over the next few days, his wife, son, and aged mother visited him on his deathbed. He told his mother, "I am satisfied to die. I have made my peace with God." Starr died on February 22, 1921, four days after the Harrison bank robbery, and his body was taken back to Oklahoma and buried at Dewey.

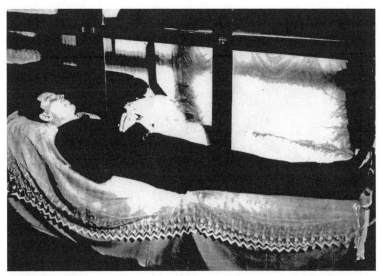

Starr's body was put on display in Harrison before being returned to Oklahoma for burial. (Courtesy Boone County Heritage Museum and the *Ozarks Mountaineer*)

20

The Eureka Springs Bank Robbery

On Tuesday evening, September 26, 1922, five desperadoes camped outside Eureka Springs, Arkansas, with plans to hold up one of the town's two banks the next day. Although George Price; his brother, Charles Price; and Si Wilson were veterans of Henry Starr's last gang, John Cowan and young Mark Hendricks were newcomers to the work of bank robbery and had just been recruited for the caper at hand.

The resort town of Eureka Springs had narrow, winding streets, and its homes and businesses were built into steep hillsides so that there were no ready exits from the rear. It was not an easy target for a bank robbery, but the gang had cased the town earlier in the day and weren't ready to give up on the plan they had hatched a couple of days earlier near Sallisaw, Oklahoma.

The next day, the bandits drove into town in a Ford Model T and parked outside the First National Bank headed downhill on Spring Street shortly after 11:00 A.M. The twenty-year-old Hendricks stayed in the car as the getaway driver while the other four men strolled into the bank with their revolvers concealed. Pausing at a service desk, they pretended to be endorsing checks as they surveyed the situation. There were five employees inside the bank, including the cashier E. T. "Toby" Smith and assistant cashier Fred Sawyer, along with four customers. The rough looks of the four newcomers and the fact that they entered the bank as a group aroused Smith's suspicion, and he edged closer to the burglar alarm when he saw them.

As soon as the bandits had located all the bank's occupants, they drew their pistols and told the captives to put up their hands. The frightened employees and customers promptly complied, but Smith touched the alarm button with his foot without being seen as he raised his hands. The alarm made no sound in the bank but, instead, sounded in three downtown businesses: the office of attorney and bank president F. O. Butt located above the bank, the Bank of Eureka Springs about a block up the street, and at the Basin Park Hotel a few doors away.

The gang herded all the hostages into the directors' room at the rear of the bank, and Wilson stood guard at the door of the room. Cowan guarded the entrance to the bank, while the Price brothers set to work gathering up all the loot they could lay their hands on.

When the burglar alarm sounded at the Basin Park Hotel, Robert Bowman, manager of the hotel, suspected it might be another accidental false alarm similar to others that had sounded in the past. He quickly phoned the bank, but when he got no answer after several rings, he decided something was wrong. He grabbed a loaded revolver, stuck it in his pocket, and started toward the bank, alerting other citizens as he passed them.

When the alarm sounded in the bank president's upstairs office, Mr. Butt also assumed it was an accident. He sent his son, John, to tell the employees below to turn the darn thing off.

At the Bank of Eureka Springs, cashier Glen Burson reached into a desk drawer and pulled out his revolver when the alarm sounded. Strolling to the front of the bank, he looked outside and noticed the unfamiliar Ford parked beside the First National Bank with a man sitting behind the wheel. His suspicions aroused, he stepped outside and started toward the scene with his gun concealed in his hip pocket. As he neared the bank, he saw Bowman hurrying from the other direction and shouting, but Burson couldn't make out what he was saying. Bowman and another man (reports differ as to whether it was young Butt or a man named Claude Arbuckle) walked into the bank, where Cowan quickly took them prisoner and forced them to stand against the wall. Assuming they were ordinary customers, though, he didn't check them for weapons.

Meanwhile, Burson passed the door of the bank without entering. A glance through the window, though, and the fidgetiness of the man behind the wheel of the Model T convinced him that a robbery was in progress. Burson crossed the street to a pool hall, took up a position in the doorway with his revolver in hand, and fired one shot at a rear tire of the Ford.

Panicking, Hendricks pulled away from the curb and roared off down Spring Street in the getaway car without waiting for his partners. Burson then opened fire in earnest at the fleeing vehicle. The Ford swerved out of control from a punctured tire and crossed the curb near the Basin Park Hotel, where Jesse Littrell, owner of a confectionary store, blasted away at the car with a shotgun. As Hendricks was trying to drive off the curb, taxi driver Sam Harmon emerged from the nearby Yellow Taxicab Company and fired another shotgun blast, which struck the young bandit in the shoulder and knocked his hands from the steering wheel. The wounded driver stomped the accelerator, but the car careened into a telephone pole and came to a halt. Littrell then took aim and fired another blast, hitting Hendricks in the chest and knocking him out of the car. Staggering to his feet, he tried to run but instead collapsed back to the cobblestone street. He was then carried to nearby Basin Park, where he lay on a bench in agony.

The robbers inside the bank had just finished gathering up $60,000 in Liberty Bonds and another $10,000 in cash when the shooting on the street outside interrupted them. What the gang had hoped would be little more than a lark had quickly turned into a desperate situation. Taking cashiers Smith and Sawyer as hostages, the robbers herded the two bank employees across the room at gunpoint and forced them to lead the way outside. Two of the gunmen walked closely behind Smith, each holding one of the hostage's arms in one hand while brandishing a revolver with the other. George Price and the fourth bandit walked behind Sawyer in similar fashion except that Price, with his gun in one hand and the loot in the other, had no hand to lay on the hostage.

Once outside, the robbers saw that their situation was even direr than they had first thought. Armed citizens were already converging on the scene, and the getaway car was gone. At first, the citizens held their fire for fear of hitting one of the hostages, but Smith and Sawyer had gone only a few steps before they bolted away from their captors, leaving the surprised gunmen exposed. Gunfire erupted as the Price brothers dashed across Spring Street toward a stone stairway that ran between two buildings down a steep hillside to a lower street. Wilson and Cowan retrieved the hostages and started to follow, but Smith and Sawyer bolted again and threw themselves face down in the street to avoid the crossfire.

Inside the bank, Robert Bowman pulled out the .45-caliber revolver he had carried into the building less than five minutes earlier and opened fire through the screen door at the retreating robbers, wounding Cowan. Attorney Joe McKimmey, perched at a window in the law office he shared with Mr. Butt, also opened fire on the bandits' rear. From the entryway of his jewelry store two doors up from the bank, Ernie Jordan fired at George Price as the fleeing bandit approached the staircase. He started to give chase but stopped when he saw the other three robbers crossing the street behind Price. Dropping to his knee, Jordan took aim and opened fire on Wilson, who was acting as a rear guard for his three sidekicks. Riddled with bullets, Wilson fell in his tracks and died on the spot.

Hearing the commotion, Constable Homer Brittain rushed to the scene. He came upon George Price as he was descending the steps and shot him in the head when the bandit ignored his order to halt. Price slumped across the handrail of the staircase and hung like a limp sack of feed; the canvas bag filled with loot dropped from his hand and rolled to the bottom of the steps.

Brittain hurried to check on the mortally wounded George Price and then climbed the steps to reinforce Jordan and the other citizens in their gun battle with the two remaining bandits. Wounded but still very much alive, Cowan had managed to cross the street and join Charlie Price near the top of the stairs, where the two were making a desperate last stand. Caught in crossfire, they were pelted with lead from all sides. They returned fire in a pitched battle that lasted almost one minute before Price finally collapsed with more than a dozen bullet wounds and Cowan fell to the cobblestone with a shattered hip. None of the citizens were seriously hurt.

After the battle, Wilson's body was taken to the Blocksom-Newton Undertaking Company. George Price died within a few minutes after being transported to the Huntington Hospital in Eureka Springs, and he, too, was removed to the morgue.

As word of the shootout spread, curious onlookers flocked to Eureka Springs throughout the afternoon to see the bloody scene of the action, to talk to those who had been involved, to gawk at the bodies of the dead robbers, and to view the wounded at the hospital. According to one Eureka Springs citizen, "Hundreds of citizens of surrounding towns and rural communities came here in motor cars, [on] horseback, and in buggies and wagons to see the dead bandits and hear the story of the sensational street fight as it was related over and over by those who participated in or witnessed it."

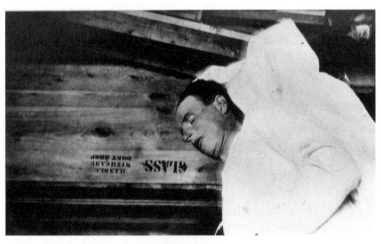

The body of Si Wilson on display after the unsuccessful bank robbery, showing that crime didn't pay in Eureka Springs. (Courtesy Eureka Springs Historical Museum/Bank of Eureka Springs Collections)

Four days later, Charlie Price died at the hospital and joined his brother at the morgue. The bodies of the Prices were taken back to Oklahoma and buried at Sallisaw. Wilson's body was never claimed and was buried in a potter's field at the Odd Fellows Cemetery in Eureka Springs. Cowan and Hendricks underwent surgery at the hospital and eventually recovered. Both pled guilty to the robbery in circuit court the following February. Cowan was sentenced from twelve to twenty-one years in the state penitentiary, and Hendricks was let off with a three-to-five-year sentence because of his youth.

In the years since the Eureka Springs bank robbery ended in disaster for the Price-Wilson gang, students of outlawry have noted several mistakes the bandits made that led to their downfall. They had picked a town built into steep hills that was not conducive to an easy escape. They had planned to stage the crime during the noon hour when few employees would be at the bank, but they arrived an hour earlier. For a getaway driver, they had brought along a green kid who panicked at

Townspeople, some displaying their weapons, gather for a photo immediately after thwarting a robbery at the First National Bank of Eureka Springs in September 1922. (Courtesy John Cross/Bank of Eureka Springs Collections)

```
AWARD FOR VALOR  PRESENTED BY
FIRST NATIONAL BANK OF EUREKA SPRINGS, ARK.
TO ERNEST A JORDAN  IN APPRECIATION OF BRAVE
AND PROMPT ATTACK ON DAYLIGHT HOLDUP MEN
SEPT. 27, 1922
```

Award for valor presented to Ernest Jordan by the First National Bank after the holdup attempt. (Courtesy Eureka Springs Historical Museum/Bank of Eureka Springs Collections)

the first sign of trouble. They failed to answer the phone in the bank when Bowman had called from the Basin Hotel after receiving the alarm. They started across the street with the hostages without a plan and let them get away too easily.

Or maybe the outlaws just forgot where they were. As a Kansas newspaperman suggested after the caper went awry, perhaps the gang didn't realize they were in Arkansas. Sitting around the camp outside Eureka Springs on the evening of September 26 plotting the robbery, maybe the "dashing bandits" thought they could sail right through the crime "like a meteor on a starry night" while the "helpless crowd of hopeless citizens stood agape." But, as the newspaperman suggested and the robbers soon found out, "That's not the way they do it in Arkansas."

In the days and weeks following the robbery attempt, the citizens who shot it out with the bandits on the streets of Eureka Springs were lauded as heroes by their friends and held up as shining examples by government officials and out-of-state newspapers. They were given monetary rewards, and Ernest Jordan received an award for valor. And today, eighty-seven years later, the community of Eureka Springs still celebrates the bravery of Jordan and his codefenders with an annual reenactment of the famous 1922 bank robbery.

21

Arkansas Tom:
The Doolin Gang's "Baddest Bad Man"

After Roy Daugherty, alias Arkansas Tom, was killed in a shootout with police in Joplin, Missouri, on August 16, 1924, approximately five thousand people filed through a local mortuary the next day to see his body. A few had been associates of Daugherty during a career of crime stretching back more than three decades. However, most, according to the *Joplin News Herald*, were "merely curious to view a man known to be of the type of fearless desperadoes who robbed, plundered and killed in the early days of outlawry when gun play was not uncommon. They knew that few of his kind have survived."

Daugherty was born about 1873 in Barry County, Missouri, and grew up there and in adjacent McDonald County in the extreme southwest corner of the state just across the border from Arkansas and Indian Territory. Daugherty left home when he was only fourteen and spent enough time in Arkansas to justify his colorful nickname before drifting into Oklahoma Territory and Texas to become a cowboy. In the spring of 1893, when he was about nineteen, he hooked up with Bill Doolin's "Wild Bunch" and starting going by the alias "Tom Jones" or just "Arkansas Tom."

In *Bill Doolin: Outlaw O. T.*, Bailey C. Hanes says that Daugherty joined the gang in time for the train robbery near Cimarron, Kansas, in early June of 1893. According to the author, when Doolin was shot in the foot by a posse that pursued the gang after the holdup, Daugherty took the outlaw leader to a hideout and then escorted him to Ingalls, Oklahoma Territory, the next day to seek medical treatment. Other sources, however, do not identify Daugherty as being among the members of the gang who robbed the train near Cimarron and suggest, instead, that Doolin happened into

Roy "Arkansas Tom" Daugherty. (Courtesy Jim Hounschell)

Daugherty's camp after he was shot and that Daugherty agreed to help the wounded man.

What is known for sure is that the outlaws retreated to Ingalls, a small town east of Stillwater where they often hid out, shortly after Daugherty joined them. U. S. Marshal E. D. Nix, charged with bringing the gang to justice, got word that the desperadoes were holed up in Ingalls and sent five of his deputies and eight other posse members to arrest them. When the thirteen lawmen arrived in two covered wagons on the morning of September 1, 1893, gang members Bill Doolin, Bill Dalton, Dan "Dynamite Dick" Clifton, George "Bitter Creek" Newcomb, George "Red Buck" Weightman, and Bill "Tulsa Jack" Blake were loitering in George Ransom's saloon. Daugherty was resting in an upstairs room of the nearby Pierce Hotel.

Deputy Dick Speed alighted from one of the wagons and saw Bitter Creek Newcomb come out of the saloon, get his horse from the adjacent livery, and start up the street. When a bystander told Speed who the man was, the deputy fired at the outlaw, and the bullet hit Newcomb's rifle, ricocheting into his leg. Hearing the shot, Daugherty hurried to the window of his hotel room and shot Speed dead as the lawman was preparing to fire a second shot at Newcomb. (Hanes says that Bitter Creek returned the deputy's fire and killed Speed himself.)

Bitter Creek mounted his horse and, under the cover of gunfire from his partners in the saloon, rode out of town amid a hail of bullets from the other deputies. After Newcomb's escape, the lawmen turned their attention to the men inside the saloon, and an all-out gun battle erupted. Fourteen-year-old Del Simmons was killed during the fierce exchange of fire by a bullet thought to have been fired by Daugherty.

The hot lead soon persuaded the outlaws in the saloon to make a run for it, so they slipped out a side door to the livery to retrieve their horses. When the lawmen shifted positions to try to cover the stable, Daugherty mortally wounded Deputy Tom Hueston with two shots from his upstairs window, and he kept firing at the deputies as his partners, several of whom were wounded, mounted up and rode out of town. During their escape, a gang member, reportedly Bill Dalton, shot and mortally wounded Deputy Lafe Shadley. A second bystander was also killed when the escaping bandits paused at the edge of town long enough to fire a final barrage at the deputies.

Trapped inside the hotel, Daugherty held the lawmen

off by himself after his partners had fled, firing shot after shot at the deputies. In return, they showered the hotel with a fusillade of gunfire that smashed bowls and splintered woodwork inside Arkansas Tom's room. At one point during the gun battle, Daugherty sent the hotelkeepers' twelve-year-old son to retrieve more ammunition, and the lad carried out the assignment without incident.

When the lone gunman learned from a local doctor that his partners had completely left the area, he fumed that he never would have thought "the boys" would desert him. (Doolin later claimed he would not have left Daugherty if he had known he was trapped inside the hotel.)

Nix's chief deputy, John Hale, soon arrived from nearby Stillwater with reinforcements and demanded Daugherty's surrender, telling the fugitive he would surely be killed if he didn't give himself up. Arkansas Tom refused at first but finally surrendered to a local preacher named Mason with the assurance that he would be protected. He was then turned over to Hale. There was talk of lynching Daugherty, but instead he was hauled to Stillwater, lodged in the city jail, and held for murder in the deaths of Speed, Hueston, and Shadley. As a precaution against vigilantism or the possibility of an attempted rescue by the Doolin gang, Daugherty's cell was closely guarded by a posse.

Then, in February of 1894, the prisoner was moved to the federal jail at Guthrie to await trial. He was brought back to Stillwater in April for arraignment and tried during the May term of court for the murder of Hueston, which the prosecutor considered the strongest case. On May 19, he was convicted of manslaughter and two days later was sentenced to fifty years in prison. Taken back to the Guthrie jail, he attempted to break out around the middle of June, but the jailer was "too quick for him." Shortly afterwards, under terms of a contract that the Territory of Oklahoma had with Kansas to house its prisoners, Daugherty was transported to the Kansas State Penitentiary to serve his sentence.

While he was cooling his heels at Lansing, all the other

members of the Wild Bunch, including Doolin himself, met violent deaths. Bill Dalton was killed near Ardmore in Indian Territory on June 8, 1894, by a deputy who was part of a posse that had been tracking him. On April 3, 1895, after robbing a train at Dover in Indian Territory, the Doolin gang was overtaken by a posse, and Tulsa Jack Blake was killed in the gun battle that ensued. Less than a month later, on May 1, 1895, Bitter Creek Newcomb and another gang member, Charlie Pierce, were killed east of Ingalls, according to most reports, by three Dunn brothers to collect the reward money offered. (There is some evidence to suggest, however, that Bitter Creek died in 1894 or 1895 from the wounds he received at Ingalls and that the man killed with Pierce was a different Newcomb. See August 2002 *Wild West* letters.) On March 4, 1896, Red Buck Weightman was killed in a gunfight with deputy marshals near Arapaho, Oklahoma Territory. On August 24 of the same year, Bill Doolin was killed by Deputy Heck Thomas's posse at Lawson, in Oklahoma Territory. Dynamite Dick Clifton, the last of Daugherty's sidekicks from the Ingalls affray, was killed by deputies on November 7, 1897, near Checotah, Indian Territory.

Although sentenced to fifty years, Daugherty didn't wait nearly that long to see the outside world again, thanks to the man who had caused his arrest. Around 1901, former marshal E. D. Nix got Daugherty temporarily released into his custody for a traveling Wild West show and took Arkansas Tom, presumably caged or under heavy guard, on a tour of Missouri and other nearby states, where the prisoner was exhibited as "Oklahoma's Most Notorious Criminal."

After his brief outing as a traveling curiosity, Daugherty was returned to Lansing and spent about six more years there. In 1907, he was transferred to the new Oklahoma State Penitentiary at McAlester.

Daugherty's brother, Samuel, a Methodist minister, had tried for years to get Roy's sentence commuted by gathering testimonies to Roy's upright character prior to his affiliation with the Doolin gang. Reverend Daugherty finally approached

Nix, who agreed to use whatever influence he might have to try to get the prisoner released. After serving three years at McAlester, Roy Daugherty was paroled in November of 1910 with the stipulation that he would report to legendary former deputy U. S. marshal Bill Tilghman at Oklahoma City. Tilghman found Daugherty a job in a store. Later, he briefly ran a restaurant in Drumright, Oklahoma. Later still, when Daugherty visited Nix at St. Louis, the former marshal got him a job as a bookkeeper.

Shortly afterwards, Nix, Tilghman, and former deputy U. S. marshal Chris Madsen formed the Eagle Film Company, and they recruited Daugherty as a technical consultant and actor for a Western they were making. Concerned that Hollywood was not accurately portraying the Old West, they tried, as much as possible, to let the actual people depicted in the movie play themselves. In addition to giving Daugherty a bit part, the three lawmen cast themselves in the movie, and outlaw Henry Starr also had a part. Released in 1915, the movie was entitled *Passing of the Oklahoma Outlaws* and included, among other events, a reenactment of the Ingalls shootout.

Apparently, though, Daugherty soon decided that being

Old bank building at Oronogo, which Daugherty robbed in 1916, as it appears today.

a crook had more appeal than playing one in the movies. On December 13, 1916, he and his cousin Albert Johnson, a former deputy sheriff in Barry County, Missouri, held up the Farmers and Miners Bank of Oronogo, Missouri, approximately fifteen miles north of Joplin. The robbers burst into the bank about 2:30 in the afternoon wearing masks, and while the taller bandit (Johnson) held the cashier at gunpoint, the smaller man (Daugherty) rifled through the cash drawers, taking over $1,700 in currency and silver. Daugherty then went into the vault and took another $750 but overlooked an additional $11,000 that was hidden there.

At some point during the robbery, Daugherty momentarily removed his mask, and he was later described by the cashier as being about 5'6" tall, weighing about 150 pounds, and having a dark complexion, dark hair, and red, sore-looking eyes. After collecting the money, the robbers forced the cashier into the vault and locked the door. The pair then made their escape in a large, gray touring car—outlaws having graduated from horses to automobiles by 1916. A third bandit named Harvey Painter served as the getaway driver. A month later, on January 13, 1917, Daugherty and Johnson, using much the same modus operandi they had used at Oronogo, teamed up with Jessie Cutler and William Massee to rob the First National Bank of Fairview, Missouri, about forty miles southeast of Joplin, in Newton County. The gang drove up to the side of the bank in a "new seven-passenger Buick touring car," and Daugherty, Johnson, and Cutler jumped out and donned masks, while Massee stayed behind the wheel with the car's engine running. The three bandits entered the bank, whipped out revolvers, and ordered the cashier to open the vault. When he did, he and his two assistants were herded inside. One of the robbers went to work gathering up all the cash he could find. After he had accumulated about $5,000, he and his sidekicks closed the vault's door on the bank employees, took off their masks, and walked nonchalantly out of the bank to the awaiting getaway car. A posse was quickly formed and gave chase but soon called off the pursuit.

In mid February of 1917, Johnson, Cutler, and Massee were taken into custody in Joplin. A fifth member of the gang, who'd been prevented from participating in the Fairview heist by his arrest the previous day, had grown angry and told what he knew because the other bandits had refused to share the spoils with him. Johnson and Cutler then gave statements implicating Daugherty and telling where he could be located.

On the evening of February 19, two Joplin detectives, William Gibson and Charles McManamy, crossed the state line to neighboring Galena, Kansas, to apprehend the fugitive. Knowing Daugherty's desperate reputation, a local citizen whom they interviewed refused at first to give them any information about the bandit's exact whereabouts but finally pointed out a house at 915 Mineral Avenue. When the detectives knocked on the door, Daugherty opened it, and the lawmen burst in before he had time to resist. Noticing a Colt revolver on a nearby table, Gibson quickly got between Daugherty and the weapon and picked it up before the fugitive could make a lunge for it. Daugherty, who was acquainted with the policeman, reportedly remarked, "I'm glad you got it, Billy. If I had beat you to it, I would have had to kill you."

Daugherty was taken back to Joplin, where he freely admitted his participation in the Oronogo and Fairview bank robberies. Despite having been implicated by Johnson and Cutler, he steadfastly clung to the thieves' code of honor and refused to say what role, if any, the other men who had been arrested had played in the crimes. He also refused to reveal where the loot from the robberies was hidden, saying that he and Johnson might have to spend long terms in prison but that Johnson's family would get to use the money. The next day, the *Joplin Globe* referred to Daugherty as the "baddest bad man," and, remarking on his stubborn reticence, said, "Talking is one of the things Arkansas Tom does not believe in."

The four men were transferred to Neosho in Newton County to answer charges related to the Fairview holdup, and all four pled guilty when they were arraigned in Circuit Court on February 26. As leader of the gang, Daugherty was sentenced to eight years in the Missouri State Penitentiary at Jefferson City. In another show of gallantry, he asked the judge to go easy on Cutler and Massee, claiming that he and Johnson had talked the pair into taking part in the robbery. Whether Daugherty's intercession swayed the judge is unknown, but Cutler was let off with a four-year sentence. Massee, on the other hand, was given six years, the same sentence as Johnson, perhaps because he, like Daugherty, had refused to cooperate with authorities.

Daugherty was transferred to Jefferson City on March 12. He had served slightly more than half of his eight-year term when the governor commuted his sentence, supposedly because of good behavior. He was released on November 11, 1921, about four and a half years after he was admitted.

His behavior inside the walls may have been exemplary enough to gain an early release, but once on the outside, it didn't take him long to drift back into a life of crime. On Saturday, November 24, 1923, Daugherty and a sidekick commandeered a taxi cab in Miami, Oklahoma, kidnapped the driver, and drove him to neighboring Commerce before releasing him.

On November 26, using the taxi as a getaway car, Daugherty and three partners, Jess Cockran, Len Brookshire, and Guy McKenzie, held up the Bank of Asbury in Asbury, Missouri, about twenty miles northwest of Joplin. Two of the men stayed in the car and two entered the bank. Presumably one of the latter was Daugherty, since the robbers followed Arkansas Tom's established mode of operation. After securing about $1,000 in cash, they locked the cashier and two other people in the vault and then started outside. As they emerged from the bank, they were met by a spate of gunfire from citizens who'd been alerted by a burglar alarm the cashier had managed to sound, but the desperadoes dodged the lead and reached the getaway car safely.

Piling into an automobile of their own, the dogged citizens gave chase as the bandit car sped west out of town, and a running gun battle erupted, with occupants of the two cars

The bank that Daugherty held up in Asbury in 1923 now serves as the post office.

exchanging fire on several different occasions. At one point, two of the robbers got out on the running boards of their car to shoot at the pursuing vehicle, which finally abandoned the chase after about fifteen miles. Despite the pitched battle, no one in either car was injured, although both vehicles were perforated with bullet holes. The *Joplin News Herald* told its readers the next day that the bank robbers had "fought their way to liberty, outwitting and out-generaling their pursuers. Gun play and bold acts of banditry that would rival some of the daring works of outlaws in the days when the James boys terrorized Missouri figured in the escape of the desperadoes."

Joplin police were notified of the Asbury holdup as soon as it happened, and motorcycle cop Clarence Allison was among those who started in pursuit of the bandits. Near Crestline, Kansas, he intercepted the gang on a rural road and exchanged fire with them as they sped by. When Allison gave chase, the robbers abandoned their car, leaving behind two bags of silver, and took to the woods on foot. Allison, also on foot, went after them. A passing motorist named Lucas drove to a nearby house to telephone authorities.

Allison found three members of the gang coming down a

ravine and got the drop on them. As he started marching his captives back toward the road, the fourth bandit, Daugherty, sneaked up behind him, stuck the barrel of his pistol against Allison's back, and told the officer to drop his gun. After the policeman complied, the march resumed with the roles now reversed. When the outlaws reached the road, they met Lucas returning to the scene and commandeered his car. Taking Allison along as a hostage, they forced the officer to drive them to Commerce, Oklahoma, where they had stolen the taxi two days earlier. At Commerce, they made Allison turn back east to an isolated spot near the Missouri state line called Devil's Promenade, where they released the captive unharmed.

By mid August of 1924, less than nine months after the Asbury robbery, two of Daugherty's partners in the caper, Cockran and Brookshire, had been tried and sentenced to prison for their parts in the crime; the third, McKenzie, had been arrested and was awaiting a preliminary hearing; and authorities were closing in on Daugherty. He had been positively identified by Allison and other witnesses from photos in the "rogue gallery" taken seven years earlier when he was convicted in the Oronogo bank robbery.

On Saturday, August 16, Joplin chief of detectives William Gibson, the same man who had arrested Daugherty in Galena seven years earlier, got word that the fugitive was staying at the home of an acquaintance named Red Snow on West Ninth Street in Joplin. About 6:30 that evening, Gibson and Detective Len VanDeventer drove to the scene in one patrol car, while Police Chief V. P. Hine and two other officers followed in another. Gibson said later that he was sure, when he left the police station, that he and his fellow officers were headed for a showdown. Amplifying the tale, he stated, "I knew we were after a man who had shot first in eighteen fatal encounters, and I expected no surrender."

Gibson and VanDeventer reached the house at 1420 West Ninth and promptly alighted from their vehicle; the other patrol car lagged behind. VanDeventer approached the front of the house, and Gibson hurried to the rear. Inside the home, Daugherty saw the policemen drive up and started to make his escape out the back door, where he was intercepted by Gibson, and both men started firing. Daugherty's first shot took "a generous chip out of the officer's straw hat," and his second one went wide before his .38-caliber automatic pistol jammed. Meanwhile, Gibson fired off four shots from his .32-caliber revolver, with three taking effect. One clipped Daugherty's right ear and grazed his head, one struck his left wrist, and another hit him in the right side.

Wounded but still very much alive, Daugherty turned and started back into the house. He was met in the front room by VanDeventer, who shot him just above the heart with a single shot from his .44-caliber revolver. Daugherty pitched onto a nearby bed and died almost instantly. The house's owner, Red Snow, was not home when the shootout occurred, but his wife, thirteen-year-old daughter, and baby were. The toddler followed at Daugherty's heels clutching at the bandit's pant legs during the gun battle, as the mother and daughter screamed hysterically, but none of the three was injured. The other police officers reached the scene too late to take part in the shootout,

The house in Joplin where police killed Daugherty in 1924 as it appears today.

and Chief Hine was later relieved of his duties for his belated arrival and for reportedly hiding in some weeds once he did reach the scene.

Daugherty's body was taken to Hurlbut Undertaking Company, where it was put on public display the next day. People turned out by the thousands to view the corpse of the legendary desperado. As the *Joplin News Herald* implied in commenting on the large turnout, most of the crowd was merely curious to see a man who was one of the last links to the lawless days of yesteryear. The Old West had been a dying era even when Daugherty had taken part in the Doolin gang's shootout at Ingalls and been sent to prison. During the next three decades, while he languished behind bars for all but a few of those thirty years, the outside world and the American way of life continued to change. By the time he was killed in Joplin in 1924, the other Doolin gang members were long gone, and the days of the Wild West were just a memory. The people who came to view his body, as the newspaper suggested, knew that men like Arkansas Tom were a vanishing breed.

22

When the Ma Barker Gang
Terrorized the Ozarks

During the Prohibition years of the 1920s and the Depression years of the 1930s, crime ran rampant and terror reigned in the heartland. Gunmen like Baby Face Nelson and Pretty Boy Floyd crisscrossed middle America, holding up banks and shooting it out with police in a desperate game of "cops and robbers." Racing across the country, many gangsters cut a swath through the Ozarks, including Bonnie and Clyde, who gunned down two policemen in Joplin, Missouri, on April 13, 1933, when their hideout was discovered in the south part of town. Of all the gangs of the era, though, none had closer ties to the Ozarks than Ma Barker and her murderous sons.

Ma was born Arizona "Arrie" Clark near Ash Grove, Missouri, northwest of Springfield about 1874 to John and Emaline Clark. At the age of eighteen, she wed thirty-three-year-old George Barker at Aurora, Missouri. Sometime after her marriage, Arrie began calling herself "Kate." While the family lived at Aurora, she gave birth to three sons: Herman, Lloyd, and Arthur (known as "Dock"). About 1903, the Barkers moved to Webb City where a fourth son, Freddie, was born in December of that year. The older boys soon earned a reputation around town for rowdiness; one of Herman's favorite frolics was riding his pony into the town's saloons in emulation of his hero, Jesse James.

The family's first serious clash with the law came in March of 1915 when the oldest son, Herman, and two other young men crashed a card game in the rear room of a grocery store on West Daugherty Street in Webb City at 3:00 A.M. on a Sunday. The group robbed the game's five participants, including the store owner, at gunpoint. When Joplin police arrested Herman and his accomplices the next day, young Barker denied his guilt,

Arrie "Ma" Barker (Courtesy Bureau of Criminal Apprehension)

and Ma helped get him released. Shortly afterwards, though, claiming she didn't want to live in such a suspicious community, she packed up and moved the family to Tulsa, Oklahoma.

In Tulsa, the Barker brothers soon fell in with other young hoodlums in the Central Park district, forming a criminal confederation that would eventually evolve into the nucleus of the Barker gang. The Barkers, though, never forgot where they came from, and they returned time and again to the Joplin-Webb City area and other southwest Missouri towns during a life of crime that spanned the next twenty years.

The family hadn't been in Tulsa long before Herman Barker struck out on his own committing petty crimes. In 1916, he was convicted of burglary and larceny in Greene County, Missouri, but escaped from the county jail at Springfield before he could be delivered to the state penitentiary.

Exhibiting a curious strain of patriotism, Arthur "Dock" Barker got himself arrested on the Fourth of July of 1918 for stealing a government-owned vehicle in Tulsa. He escaped and fled to Joplin, where he was recaptured in 1920 and returned to Tulsa. He escaped again, was rearrested, and was discharged by court order in 1921. Then in 1922, he was sentenced to life in the Oklahoma State Penitentiary at McAlester for killing a night watchman at a Tulsa hospital.

Lloyd "Red" Barker was convicted of mail robbery at Baxter Springs, Kansas, in January of 1922 and was sent to Leavenworth to serve a twenty-five-year sentence.

As a teenager, the youngest brother, Fred Barker, returned to the Joplin area, where he stayed temporarily on a chicken ranch owned by Herb Farmer, a former Webb City neighbor who had just been released from the McAlester prison. In September of 1922, Fred was arrested in Miami, Oklahoma, for questioning. After his release, he went on a crime spree that finally resulted in his arrest at Winfield, Kansas, for burglary and grand larceny. He was convicted and sentenced to five to ten years in the state prison at Lansing.

In September of 1926, Herman Barker, still on the lam from Missouri, was charged with robbing the county attorney at Miami, Oklahoma. Released on bond, Barker joined up with Ray Terrill, a sidekick from the old "Central Park Gang," and set out on a series of bank robberies in Oklahoma, Arkansas, Missouri, and Kansas.

In the wee hours of the morning on Monday, January 17, 1927, the gang was interrupted in the process of robbing the First National Bank of Jasper, Missouri, when a baker who noticed suspicious activity at the bank as he arrived for work in a nearby building notified authorities. The town marshal quickly organized a group of citizens, who tried to surprise the robbers at the rear of the bank where they were attempting to load the safe into a stolen truck. The gang, however, was alerted to the posse and made their escape through the unguarded front entrance of the bank. Barker and Terrill roared off to the south while three other members of the gang fled west in a second getaway car. The town marshal fired a shot through the window of one of the vehicles, but no one was hurt.

As their accomplices raced for the Kansas border, Barker and Terrill returned to their hideout at 602 East Main Street in Carterville, Missouri. Within an hour, officers from Joplin and Webb City surrounded the place, which had been under surveillance since the previous day. As they closed in, Barker dashed out the back door. A Joplin detective brought the fugitive down with several blasts from a sawed-off shotgun after Barker refused the officer's command to halt. Meanwhile, Terrill exchanged fire with the other officers before surrendering unharmed.

Barker was taken to Joplin's St. John's Hospital, where he identified himself as R. L. Douglas and refused to give any details about the gang's activities, saying, "There's nothing to tell." When prosecuting attorney Frank Birkhead came to the hospital to interview him, Barker looked up from his bed and said, "I'm pleased to meet you; I sure am."

The next day Barker's true identity was discovered, and both Terrill and Barker were revealed as dangerous criminals who were, according to the January 18, 1927, *Joplin News Herald,* "wanted in connection with no fewer than a dozen bank robberies and burglaries in Oklahoma." The same day a safe from a bank at Rogersville, Missouri, which had been robbed the previous Saturday night, was dragged from a creek not far from the house where the two desperados had been captured, thus linking them to the earlier bank job as well. Terrill was returned to Oklahoma to serve out a prior bank robbery conviction while Herman Barker was extradited to Fayetteville, Arkansas, to face a charge of robbing a bank at Westfork. However, both men escaped within a matter of weeks.

A few months later, in early August of 1927, Herman killed a lawman in Wyoming after holding up a bank there. Then on August 29, after a stick-up in Newton, Kansas, he killed another officer in a gun battle with Wichita police. Seriously wounded, Herman Barker turned his weapon on himself and committed suicide. George and Kate Barker buried their oldest son in a cemetery near Welch, Oklahoma.

Headstone of Herman Barker at Williams-Timberhill Cemetery near Welch, Oklahoma. (Other family members are buried in unmarked graves beside him.)

About 1928, Kate and George Barker separated, apparently over Ma's penchant for dating other men. George returned to Webb City, and Ma moved in with a drunken billboard painter named Arthur Dunlop.

Fred Barker was paroled from the Kansas prison in March of 1931 and moved into a house at 701 Byers in Joplin with another ex-con. A couple of months later, Alvin Karpis, a burglar and con man Fred had gotten to know in prison, was also paroled, and he contacted Ma Barker in Tulsa. Fred soon joined Karpis, and they set out on a string of small-time burglaries, mainly in Oklahoma.

Later in the year, Fred and Ma Barker and Arthur Dunlop moved to a rented farm near Thayer, Missouri, where they were soon joined by Karpis. On October 7, 1931, Fred Barker, Alvin Karpis, and two other gang members robbed the People's Bank of Mountain View, Missouri, and in November, Fred killed a night constable at Pocahontas, Arkansas.

Then on the evening of December 17, the gang burglarized McCallon's Clothing Store at West Plains. On the morning of the nineteenth, Fred Barker and Alvin Karpis drove a 1931 blue DeSoto into Davidson's Garage in West Plains to get two flats fixed. The mechanic noticed that the tread of the tires matched that left at the clothing store. He notified his boss, Carac Davidson, who walked to the clothing store to inform the owner, C. C. McCallon, of his suspicions. As Davidson was returning to the garage, he saw the Howell County sheriff, C. R. Kelly, coming out of the post office across the street, and he reiterated his suspicions to the officer. Sheriff Kelly walked into the garage to investigate. When he opened the door of the Desoto, where the two outlaws were still seated, Barker stepped out and fired four shots at the sheriff at point-blank range. Two hit him in the left arm and two in the heart, killing him instantly.

Karpis drove the DeSoto out of the garage and roared down Main Street. A bystander named Dutch James grabbed a repeating twenty-two rifle from his nearby car and fired five shots at the fleeing vehicle but to no avail. Meanwhile, Barker ran out of the garage on foot brandishing his revolver and darted down a side street. Later a red scarf he had been wearing was found on nearby Washington Avenue, but by then, he had disappeared in the heavy Saturday-morning traffic.

Area officers raided the farm near Thayer but only found photos and letters identifying the former occupants and some of the goods stolen from McCallon's store. The sheriff's widow, succeeding her husband as sheriff, offered a reward for the arrest of the gang, including $100 for "Old Lady Arrie Barker." This apparently was the first official recognition of Ma Barker.

The gang fled to Joplin, where their old friend Herb Farmer advised them to go to St. Paul, Minnesota. In St. Paul, Fred Barker and Alvin Karpis made some important underworld connections, and the Barker-Karpis gang rose in notoriety. In the spring of 1932, Dunlop was killed as a suspected informer, and the gang returned to the Kansas City area. On June 17, Fred Barker, Alvin Karpis, and other members of the gang held up the Citizens National Bank at Fort Scott, Kansas.

In September of 1932, Arthur "Dock" Barker was paroled from his life sentence in the Oklahoma State Prison. After spending a few days with his father in Webb City, Dock joined the gang, and over the next two and half years, the Barker-Karpis gang carried out a string of bank robberies, murders, and kidnappings that landed members on the FBI's most-wanted list.

In early January of 1935, Dock Barker was captured in Chicago, and a few days later, on January 16, FBI agents moved in on a house at Ocklawaha, Florida, where Fred and Ma were holed up. A four-hour gun battle, during which agents pelted the house with over 1,500 rounds of ammunition, ensued. Afterwards, Fred was found dead in an upstairs room with fourteen bullets in him, and Ma lay dead beside him with a single gunshot wound. Also found were numerous high-powered weapons, a large quantity of ammunition, and more than $14,000 in cash.

Although the evidence seems to suggest otherwise, it's unclear whether Ma actually participated in the shootout. Despite popular myth to the contrary, Ma was never the ringleader of the Barker gang or its behind-the-scenes mastermind. What she was, was a doting, overprotective mother whose villainous sons could do no wrong in her eyes.

George Barker brought the bodies of his wife and son home to rest in the same cemetery at Welch, Oklahoma, where Herman was buried. Dock was sent to Leavenworth, then Alcatraz, and was shot to death on January 13, 1939, during an escape attempt. His father brought his body back to Welch, too. George Barker died in Webb City in 1941, and he was also buried at Welch. Paroled in 1938 from his sentence for mail robbery, Lloyd Barker went straight and served in the army during World War II, but in 1949, his wife killed him with a shotgun blast in Colorado and there was no one left to bring his body home.

23

Bloody Day in Brookline:
The Young Brothers Massacre

On the late afternoon of Saturday, January 2, 1932, ten Greene County, Missouri, law officers closed in on the Brookline farmhouse where twenty-eight-year-old fugitive and ex-convict Harry Young was holed up with his thirty-four-year-old brother Jennings. Not expecting the Young brothers to put up much of a fight, the officers considered their mission a bit of a lark. They had even allowed a civilian to come along for the ride. However, they had grossly underestimated the desperate character of the men they were about to face. Unknown to them, Harry Young had been heard to say, during the two and a half years he had been on the run, that he meant to avoid going back to prison at all costs and would not be taken alive. At least in this case, Harry Young was true to his word. By the time the showdown at the farmhouse was over, six of the ten lawmen lay dead in what still ranks as the deadliest shootout for policemen in American law enforcement history.

The Young brothers were part of a large Ozarks family that included their parents, J. D. and Willie; brothers Jarrett, Oscar, and Paul; and sisters Lou Rettie, Mary Ellen, Gladys, Florence, Lorena, and Vinita. Most of the children were born in Christian County, Missouri, near Ozark. The youngest three, including Harry, were born after the family moved to Tillman County, Oklahoma, in 1902.

The Youngs returned to Christian County in 1917, and the following year they bought a farm in Greene County west of Springfield near Brookline. Later the same year, the Young brothers first ran afoul of the law when Jennings and older brother Paul were charged with burglarizing two stores in Ozark and one in Nixa and were implicated in several other burglaries. They were convicted and sentenced to ten years in the Missouri state prison but were paroled in 1922.

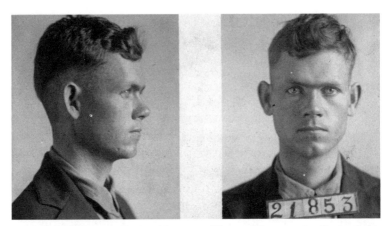

Mug shot of Jennings Young. (Courtesy History Museum for Springfield-Greene County)

If the purpose of incarceration is rehabilitation, it didn't take in the case of Jennings Young. Shortly after his release, Jennings was charged with burglarizing a hardware store in Billings, but the case ended in a hung jury. Then in April of 1924, he and other members of his family were charged with breaking into and stealing merchandise from a freight car in Springfield. Only Jennings was indicted. He was convicted and sentenced to three years in the federal penitentiary at Leavenworth.

Harry Young promptly took up where his brother had left off. In 1925, Harry was charged in Greene County with altering a vehicle motor number and was fined $100. His career in crime escalated from there, as he was charged during the next year with a string of crimes including receiving stolen property, stealing a car from a farmer near Republic, and burglarizing a store in Republic. In each case, he was released on bond, but in early 1927, he was charged with burglarizing a service station in Springfield and failed to make bond. When the four cases were heard in April of that year, charges in the first three were dismissed, but Harry pled guilty to larceny in the service station case and was sentenced to three years in the penitentiary. He was paroled after serving a year and a half.

On the night of June 2, 1929, twenty months after his release, Harry and a young man named Orey Lafollette were drinking and carousing in Republic in full view of night watchman Mark Noe. Late in the evening, as the pair grew more boisterous and started roaring up and down Main Street in a 1926 Ford Coupe, Noe decided it was time to put a halt to their revelry. When the car stopped in front of a café, Noe approached and told the men they were under arrest. He got into the car with the two men and ordered Harry to drive to the home of a local justice of the peace, but Harry drove only a short distance down Main Street before brandishing a gun. As he and the lawman struggled over the weapon, it went off, striking Noe. During the scuffle, Harry's companion managed to slide out of the vehicle, and as Lafollette started walking away, Harry shot Noe twice more for good measure. He then drove the body outside town and dumped it in a roadside ditch. Harry fled the territory, and a reward for his capture was posted. Rumors placed him in Wichita, Tulsa, and various other locations over the next two and a half years, as he remained on the run.

Harry's brother Jennings, meanwhile, after being released from Leavenworth, had managed to stay out of jail for a couple of years. However, in early 1930, the law once again caught up with him when he was indicted in Tarrant County, Texas, for the theft and transport of automobiles in interstate commerce. Specifically, he was charged with stealing two cars in San Diego, California, and one in Lawton, Oklahoma (near where the Youngs had once lived), and taking them to Fort Worth, Texas, to sell. Jennings pled guilty and was sent back to Leavenworth in April of 1930 to serve a two-year term. He was discharged on November 7, 1931, and quickly hooked up with his fugitive brother.

On the late night of Wednesday, December 30, 1931, he and Harry pulled into the Young family's Brookline farmhouse, having traveled together from Texas in separate vehicles. The next morning the brothers tried to sell one of the cars, a stolen Ford sedan, to an Aurora automobile dealer,

Vinita and Lorena Young were arrested when they tried to sell a car their murderous brothers had stolen. (Courtesy History Museum for Springfield-Greene County)

but he told them they needed solid references. Jennings and Harry then enlisted the help of their sisters Lorena and Vinita. On Thursday afternoon, Lorena tried to sell the stolen vehicle, registered to "J. P. Young," to car dealer Clyde Medley on McDaniel Street in Springfield, but he told her she could not sell a car that was not registered in her name. The Youngs then went to a notary public to have the title transferred to Lorena. The next day, Friday, January 1, 1932, Lorena and Vinita returned to Medley's business, but the dealer again put them off. He told Lorena he couldn't come up with the asked-for $250 in cash on New Year's Day and suggested she return the following day.

Suspecting that the car was stolen, Medley called the police, and the next day, Saturday, January 2, two officers staked out the car lot. When Lorena and Vinita showed up near midafternoon to once again try to sell the stolen car, they were arrested and taken to the city jail. At first they denied that Jennings and Harry were anywhere in the vicinity, but they soon admitted that their brothers were alone at the family farmhouse near Brookline, because they had dropped their mother and other family members off at a home in Springfield.

Although the attempt to sell the stolen car was a city matter, Springfield police chief Ed Waddle thought it best to involve the sheriff's department, since the Young farmhouse was located in the sheriff's jurisdiction and since Harry Young was wanted for killing Mark Noe in Republic. Sheriff Marcell Hendrix arrived at the police station around 3:30 P.M. with his deputy sheriff Wiley Mashburn and special deputy Ollie Crosswhite. Detective Virgil Johnson jumped into the car with them. Police officers Tony Oliver, Sid Meadows, Ben Bilyeu, and Charley Houser took off in another car. As the two vehicles drove off, policemen Frank Pike and Owen Brown pulled up in a third car. Civilian B. G. Wegman hopped in the car with them, and they, like the first two carloads, tore off toward Brookline.

The lawmen, thinking that their sheer numbers were

enough to ensure that the capture of two small-time car thieves would be a relatively routine arrest, carried only pistols and a couple of tear-gas canisters. Unknown to the officers as they pulled up to the farmhouse on Haseltine Road west of Springfield, Jennings and Harry Young, holed up inside, were armed with a Winchester automatic shotgun and a Remington repeating rifle.

It was now 4:00 P.M., and all was quiet as the lawmen got out of their cars and surrounded the house. It appeared as though Lorena and Vinita might have given the police faulty intelligence and that no one was home. Sid Meadows, Virgil Johnson, and Ben Bilyeu stepped onto the front porch, knocked on the door, and shouted Jennings's and Harry's names. Still no answer. Ollie Crosswhite and Charley Houser tried the kitchen door at the side of the house with no success and then joined the three men at the front. Crosswhite pressed his face up against the windowpane to try to peer inside. He couldn't see anybody, but he swore he heard footsteps coming from somewhere inside the house. Using a skeleton key, Houser tried to open the front door, but it was locked from the inside. Johnson threw a tear-gas canister at a second-story window, but it bounced off the frame.

Sheriff Hendrix, swearing that he wasn't leaving until he found out for sure whether the Young brothers were there, headed toward the back door, followed by Wiley Mashburn and Frank Pike. The sheriff kicked in the door, and as soon as it flew open, a shotgun exploded. A load of buckshot hit Hendrix squarely in the chest. The blast knocked him backwards out of the doorway, and he fell to the ground dead. A second blast smashed into Wiley Mashburn's face, nearly knocking his eye out. He staggered back and slumped to the ground but didn't die for several hours. Buckshot from the second blast also struck Frank Pike in the arm, convincing him to retreat. He rejoined the others at the front of the house and told them what had happened. Incensed by the news, the remaining officers fruitlessly poured a fusillade of pistol fire into the house as they sought shelter behind trees and outbuildings, and Johnson fired another tear-gas canister toward the house. It, like the first, bounced off a window frame without doing any damage.

The Young brothers returned fire, and a rifle bullet from an upstairs window struck Houser in the head, killing him instantly. Meadows peeked out from behind a tree and took a slug in the forehead. Then Crosswhite was hit in the head by a shotgun blast as he crawled toward a storm cellar behind the house.

Tony Oliver, chief of detectives, ordered Johnson to go for help. Bilyeu and Wegman jumped into the car with Johnson, leaving Oliver, Pike, and Brown as the only officers still on the scene who weren't dead or dying. A barrage of shotgun pellets splintered the maple tree behind which Oliver had sought shelter, and when one finally pierced his coat, he stepped to the other side of the tree. A rifle shot immediately tore into his shoulder. As he started to retreat to the police car at his rear, another rifle bullet ripped into his back. He staggered to the car, collapsed, and died. Out of ammunition, Pike and Brown made a dash to safety across an open field, dodging gunfire the whole way.

As the two officers awaited reinforcements, the Young brothers escaped and made their way to Springfield, where they stole a car and headed for Houston, Texas. A nationwide manhunt was launched, and Houston police located and trapped the fugitives in a boarding house three days later. This time the lawmen were the ones with the high-powered arms. The Young brothers, having abandoned their stolen car with the murder weapons in it, carried only pistols. After briefly exchanging fire with the policemen, Jennings and Harry Young shot each other in a suicide pact as the officers closed in. A Springfield undertaker made a hurried trip to Houston to bring back their bodies, but a large crowd met the returning hearse to proclaim that the killers shouldn't be interred in Greene County. The undertaker turned back, and the Young brothers were buried in Joplin's Fairview Cemetery. A stone marker, placed by their sister Vinita some years later, marks

Vinita placed a headstone on her brothers' graves at Fairview Cemetery in Joplin years after their deaths.

the spot, but probably few people passing the cemetery each day along Joplin's Maiden Lane suspect that two of America's most notorious criminals are buried there.

24

The Dark Day Bonnie
and Clyde Terrorized Joplin

During Prohibition, gangs of deadly outlaws, spurred partially by the lucrative bootlegging trade, traveled the United States, particularly the Midwest, terrorizing the American people. One such gang was known as the Barrow gang and featured Bonnie Parker and Clyde Barrow, who were immortalized by the 1967 movie starring Faye Dunaway and Warren Beatty entitled *Bonnie and Clyde*. On April 13, 1933, the Barrow gang left its mark on Joplin, Missouri.

Marvin Ivan "Buck" Barrow was released from the Texas State Penitentiary at Huntsville on March 22, 1933. He had just served two years of a five-year sentence for a burglary he had committed with his brother Clyde. Clyde had not been captured and was now the leader of the notorious gang. Buck had recently married Blanch Caldwell and, according to many accounts, wanted to start a new life. He only wanted to see Clyde to try to talk his brother into turning himself in to authorities and going straight. A meeting was arranged to take place in Joplin.

Buck rented an apartment at 3347½ Oak Ridge Drive from Paul Freeman by posing as J. W. Callahan, an engineer from Minnesota. The apartment consisted of a living room, two bedrooms, a bathroom, and a kitchen. The limestone building had two stories with the living quarters upstairs and a two-car garage below. The only entrances to the apartment were on the south side, the same side as the garage door, and from the inside of the garage, where a stairway led directly upstairs. This set-up was ideal for a gang of outlaws, because the occupants of the apartment could unload weapons and other contraband or pile into the vehicle for a getaway without

Photo of Bonnie Parker developed from film left behind at the Joplin apartment. (Courtesy the *Joplin Globe*)

being seen. In addition, the apartment was located on the very south edge of Joplin only two blocks from Main Street.

At the reunion were Clyde Barrow, Bonnie Parker, Buck and Blanch Barrow, and W. D. Jones, a friend and accomplice of Clyde and Bonnie. Parked in the garage were two stolen vehicles, a Ford V-8 and a Ford Coupe. Clyde also rented a garage at 3339 Oak Ridge Drive from Sam Langford for Buck's Ford sedan, which his sister had bought for Buck upon his release from prison. This car was the one mostly used by the gang during its stay in Joplin, as the garage doors at the apartment were rarely opened.

For about two weeks, the gang simply took it easy. Bonnie wrote poetry and did most of the cooking with help from Blanch. The men relaxed and played cards. As the gang began to run low on funds, however, it soon resorted to crime, including a burglary of the Neosho Milling Company.

The increased activity at the apartment drew the attention of neighbors. One noticed that different license plates were being used on the same vehicle and reported the suspicious activity to the highway patrol office (then located at Twentieth and Main). Two officers, George Kohler and Walter Grammer, were sent to the location, and they found that the license plate on Buck's car was registered in the name of Barrow, while the apartment had been rented by a man calling himself Callahan. The two suspected that the occupants of the apartment were either bootleggers or burglars.

The two patrolmen enlisted the aid of Joplin Police detectives Harry McGinnis and Thomas DeGraff, and Newton County constable J. W. Harryman was also contacted to obtain a warrant, since the Oak Ridge Drive address was located in Newton County. The five met at the patrol station and set out, the troopers in one car and the other three men in a city police car.

It was Tuesday, April 12, at 4:00 P.M. when the police cars arrived at the apartment. Clyde and W. D. had just returned from a scouting expedition and were still in the garage. Upstairs Bonnie was cooking, Blanch was playing solitaire, and Buck was asleep. When he saw the law enforcement vehicles, W. D. handed Clyde a sawed-off shotgun and hurried upstairs to alert the others.

The men in the Joplin police car spotted Clyde in the doorway of the garage just inside the partly open door. DeGraff, the driver, whipped the car into the driveway and stopped just west of the apartment building. Harryman, the front seat passenger, leaped from the car and rushed toward the garage to try to intercept Clyde before he closed the door.

Clyde opened fire with the shotgun, and Harryman, spattered with lead, plunged headlong inside the doorway of

Photo of Clyde Barrow from film left behind at the Joplin apartment. (Courtesy the *Joplin Globe.*)

the garage. McGinnis, in the rear of the two-door car, pushed up the front seat and started to get out. Clyde, who had momentarily ducked for cover, reappeared in the doorway and fired again. McGinnis reeled against the vehicle and returned fire. DeGraff opened fire from the driver's seat and got outside, using the car as a shield.

By now, Bonnie and W. D. Jones had opened fire from the windows of the apartment with powerful automatic weapons. McGinnis was shot again, and he collapsed, his arm nearly severed. DeGraff ran to him, picked up his revolver, and took cover behind the east corner of the apartment building.

House where the Joplin shootout occurred as it appears today.

Trooper Grammer, meanwhile, had rushed to the west side of the building, and Kohler, using the corner of a nearby home as a shield, was firing from his position.

Chaos reigned outside the building. The officers had gone to the home not expecting violence and certainly not a total shootout; they had been caught by surprise, because they had no idea who they were dealing with. DeGraff yelled to Grammer to get to a telephone and call for help. Grammer rushed to a nearby phone and called the police station for reinforcements.

The scene inside the apartment was hectic as well. As reported later by the desperadoes themselves, Blanch ran screaming down the stairs and out into the yard with her pet dog yapping at her heels. Startled by her sudden appearance, the police held their fire as the unarmed woman fled through the neighboring streets.

With shots still being fired from the apartment, DeGraff ran to the back (north) side of the building to try to gain entrance. Only Kohler remained in front, and he had a single bullet left. Since he was the only visible officer, the gunmen inside directed their fire at him. As he moved backward, he tripped and fell, and Clyde, thinking the officer had been hit, called for W. D. to come to the front of the garage so they could make their escape. As Jones appeared, Kohler, recovering from his fall, took aim and fired his last shot, wounding Jones slightly in the head. Kohler then charged for safety.

Clyde opened the garage doors, and Bonnie and Buck dived into the Ford V-8. Clyde climbed into the driver's seat and noticed blood on his shirt from a superficial chest wound. Able to feel the bullet, he demanded that Bonnie dig it out. Bonnie whipped out a hairpin and quickly dug out the bullet, which had apparently ricocheted off something to cause the wound.

Enraged from the wound, Clyde climbed back out of the car carrying either a machine gun or a shotgun (according to differing reports). Bonnie yelled for him to get back in the car, but he vowed first to get the "rat" who had shot him. Clyde fired away at DeGraff, who had momentarily reappeared but quickly ducked behind a wall.

Finally, his rage subsided sufficiently for Clyde to turn his attention once again to making his escape, but the driveway was still blocked by the police car. W. D. Jones darted to the obstructing vehicle, released the brake, and gave it a shove that sent it down the sloping driveway and into a tree. Clyde slid once again behind the wheel of the Ford and rolled the car out of the drive as W. D. Jones fired away with a machine gun from the passenger side.

Clyde and his passengers found Blanch near Main Street, where she was reportedly still running and sobbing, carrying her little dog. They picked her up and headed south on Main Street at a high rate of speed. The fleeing car approached the Redings Mill Bridge across Shoal Creek south of Joplin at such a high speed that, according to a nearby service station attendant, it narrowly missed plunging into the creek as it negotiated a sharp turn leading onto the bridge. The occupants then smiled and waved gleefully at the attendant as the car sped south and ultimately made its escape through Seneca, west through Oklahoma, and into Texas.

Back in Joplin, the two downed officers, Detective

McGinnis and Constable Harryman, were rushed to the hospital. Harryman, however, died en route, and McGinnis succumbed later that night.

A search of the apartment at 3347½ Oak Ridge Drive turned up eight guns: three revolvers, four rifles, and a machine gun. Four diamonds were found and identified as having come from the Neosho Milling Company. Buck and Blanch's marriage certificate was found along with Buck's pardon papers from the governor. Also among the papers found in the apartment was a poem Bonnie had been writing entitled "The Story of Suicide Sal."

From the items found, the bandits were quickly identified, and telegrams were sent to every city for hundreds of miles in every direction to be on the lookout. The Barrow gang, though, avoided capture and continued to rob and murder for another year. Buck and Blanch were captured in a shootout in Iowa on July 24, 1933, but it was not until May 23, 1934, that Texas Rangers ambushed and killed Bonnie and Clyde in Louisiana.

The apartment building where the infamous shootout occurred stood inconspicuously in a quiet residential neighborhood in the south part of Joplin for many years, its status as the scene of a bloody shootout unknown even to many local citizens. A new owner bought the property a few years ago and has refurbished it. The Missouri Advisory Council on Historic Preservation has approved an application to have the house designated as a historic site, and the owner is still awaiting review from the National Register of Historic Places. The recent renovations have preserved the historical integrity of the building, and a close inspection may still reveal bullet holes in the walls and garage doors of the structure, a testimony to the building's violent past. Moreover, despite recent publicity surrounding the site, to casual passersby the small apartment looks totally innocuous, and unsuspecting observers would never guess that a bloody cops-and-robbers shootout that left two men dead took place at the scene seventy-six years ago.

25

Badman Bill Cook

On Christmas day of 1950, twenty-two-year-old ex-convict Bill Cook got drunk at Blythe, California, where he was employed as a dishwasher, and he hitchhiked to El Paso, Texas. He crossed the border into Juarez, looking for a Mexican girl to smuggle back into the United States. He found a girl, but she wouldn't go with him. So, he started north by himself toward his hometown of Joplin, Missouri.

At Lubbock, Texas, the droopy-eyed Cook caught a ride with a man named Lee Archer, who drove him to the Oklahoma City area. There, on December 30, Cook brandished a gun, stole one hundred dollars from Archer, and forced him out of his car. Aware that police would soon have a description of the stolen vehicle, Cook drove only a short distance before abandoning it along the road.

As Cook started trying to hitch another ride, Carl Mosser; his wife, Thelma; and their three children happened along Route 66 in a 1949 two-door Chevrolet on their way from their home in Atwood, Illinois, to visit Mosser's brother in Albuquerque, New Mexico. Cook stood in the highway to flag the car down, then flourished his gun. He jumped in the vehicle and ordered the startled Mosser to drive to Oklahoma City.

From there the trail coursed to Wichita Falls, Texas, where Cook forced Mosser to accompany him into a grocery store to buy food while the rest of the frightened family stayed in the car. Inside the store, Mosser jumped Cook, and, as the two men struggled, he shouted that he and his family were in danger. Cook pulled out his gun and forced Mosser back into the car. The storekeeper, under the impression that the two were either partners in a botched hold-up attempt or involved

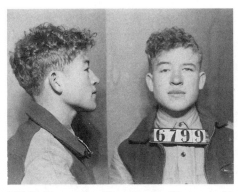

Bill Cook's mug shot. (Courtesy Jim Hounschell)

in a private squabble, passed the incident off with scarcely a second thought.

After learning the Mossers' destination, Cook told the father to drive toward Albuquerque, but at Carlsbad, New Mexico, Mosser tried to escape again. Cook warned him that he would kill the entire family if there were any more problems, and he ordered Mosser to drive instead to El Paso. From there the pell-mell journey backtracked to Houston, Texas, then to Winthrop, Arkansas, where the group stopped at a grocery for food. Late on the afternoon of New Year's Day 1951, they headed north along Highway 71 toward Joplin with Carl Mosser still at the wheel.

They skirted the south edge of town upon entering Joplin in the early-morning hours of January 2 and stopped in the southwest limits of the city near Thirty-second Street on Maiden Lane, which served as a portion of Highway 166 through the town. According to Cook's later confession, he planned to abandon the Mossers at the scene, and they had "agreed" to be tied up in order to give Cook time to make his getaway. Cook bound and gagged the mother and her seven-year-old son Ronald Dean and started to tie up Carl Mosser when a Joplin police car drove by.

Patrolmen Nathan Keaton and Floyd Cline noticed a vehicle with Illinois license plates parked at the side of the road, and they turned around at Twenty-sixth Street to make another pass. This time, according to Cline, "We threw our lights on the car, but when we saw there were children in it, we didn't suspect anything, so we drove on."

The taillights on the police car were not yet out of sight when Mrs. Mosser and her kids grew hysterical and started screaming. Cook promptly leveled his .32-caliber revolver and started firing. He shot Thelma Mosser once through the chest; put the gun to her husband's head and pulled the trigger; riddled seven-year-old Ronald Dean with bullets; and shot the two younger children, Gary Carl, five, and Pamela Sue, three, once each through the heart.

Cook then took the wheel and drove around Joplin for about an hour with his gruesome cargo, contemplating his next move. Around 3:00 A.M., he drove to an old abandoned mine shaft in the northwest part of town, near where he had grown up.

After Cook's mother died when the boy was just five years old, he and his seven siblings (four older and three younger) were left to fend for themselves. Their elderly father, William E. Cook Sr., who lived in a one-room shanty in the small mining village of Chitwood at the northwest edge of Joplin, apparently had neither the means nor the inclination to take care of eight kids. About a year after the mother's death, juvenile authorities found the children living in the cave-in of an old mine with the eldest sibling, Bill's fourteen-year-old sister, in charge. The father had left them there but periodically dropped by to bring food.

For the next several years, Bill bounced back and forth between foster homes and the home of his older sister, who had gotten married. One of Bill's foster mothers adopted him when he was ten, but he became incorrigible and left home when he was twelve, complaining to juvenile authorities that the foster mother had sold his clothes and that a bicycle she had bought him for Christmas had been taken by a credit company. The juvenile officers told Bill he had to agree to live where he was placed and go to school or else go to a reformatory. He chose the reformatory.

After ten months at the Boonville reformatory in upstate Missouri, "Cockeye Cook," as he was called there, came back to Joplin in 1941 and lived briefly with his sister but mostly wherever he happened to land. In 1943, just after his fifteenth birthday, he held up a taxi driver at gunpoint,

Bill Cook dressed in his Sunday best. (Courtesy Jim Hounschell)

then hit the cabby up beside the head with a blackjack and left. The next day the cab driver spotted Cook in downtown Joplin and helped secure his arrest.

This time Bill was sentenced to five years in the reformatory, where he earned a reputation as a troublemaker. In 1946, he escaped and returned to Joplin but was recaptured a few months later. "Cookie," as he was sometimes called, was now sent to an intermediate reformatory near Jefferson City on a car-tampering charge resulting from his attempt to steal an automobile after his escape. When he again tried to escape, the eighteen-year-old Cook was promptly transferred to the state penitentiary as incorrigible.

Released in June of 1950, he came back to Joplin sporting a two-inch scar on his upper lip and several tattoos, including the word "HARD" spelled out on the knuckles of his left hand. It was reported that he meant to have "LUCK" tattooed on his other hand but never got around to it.

One day in November, Bill went to his father and told the elder man he meant to "live by the gun" from now on. He wanted his father to provide him with alibis by vouching for his whereabouts whenever he was suspected of a crime. His father refused, and the two men parted for the final time. Next, Bill tried to enlist a former prison buddy, Harold Martin of Joplin, in a partnership of crime. He took Martin to the old mine shaft off West Fourth Street and threatened to kill him and toss his body in if he didn't cooperate, but Martin managed to escape. Shortly afterwards, Cook left Joplin headed for California.

Now, though, less than two months later, he was back in town hauling five dead bodies, and he had returned to his old neighborhood to dispose of the evidence of his bloody crime. He pulled up to the mine shaft along a dirt alley north of the 2100 block of West Fourth Street. Located only a couple of blocks from the home of the woman who had adopted him, it was the same shaft into which he had threatened to throw Harold Martin. Cook pried off the two boards covering the shaft, carried the bodies one by one from the car, and dumped them into the dark depths of the

The Carl Mosser family, victims of Bill Cook. (Courtesy Jim Hounschell)

water that filled the one hundred-foot pit beyond the halfway point.

After replacing the boards, Cook jumped back in the Mossers' car and took off heading west. At Tulsa, he abandoned the vehicle in the weeds of a back road on the outskirts of town but not before a passerby got a good look at him standing beside the car.

After police found the deserted automobile on January 3 with bloody clothes in it and bullet holes in the seats, it didn't take long before Bill Cook became the chief suspect in the disappearance and presumed murder of the Mossers. A receipt for a gun purchased at a St. Louis pawnshop bearing Cook's name was found in Lee Archer's abandoned vehicle near Oklahoma City, and an eyewitness identified the man who had abandoned it as the same man who had waylaid the occupants of a blue 1949 Chevy with Illinois license plates. When a picture of Bill Cook was circulated, Archer recognized Cook as the man who had robbed him, and both the witness who had seen Cook flag down the Mossers and the one who had seen him abandon their car at Tulsa identified him as well.

The search for the missing Mosser family was concentrated in Oklahoma. Under the supposition that Cook might have brought the Mossers back to his hometown, though, a search was soon undertaken in the Joplin area also.

Meanwhile, Cook made his way back to California by bus and by hitchhiking. At Blythe, he kidnapped a deputy sheriff named Homer Waldrip when the lawman, the husband of a waitress in the café where Cook had worked, found the fugitive at the same motel where he had stayed while employed as a dishwasher. Cook forced Waldrip at gunpoint to drive him south of town in his squad car. Along the way,

Entrance to Peace Church Cemetery at the north edge of Joplin, where Bill Cook is buried in an unmarked grave.

Cook confessed to killing the Mossers and claimed to have killed seven people in all.

About forty miles below Blythe, Cook left the deputy tied up at the side of the road and took his patrol car. A few miles farther south, he turned on the car's red light and pulled over a salesman named Robert Dewey. Cook walked up to the car and shot the man through the head when he reached for a dropped cigarette. Cook stuffed the body into the patrol car and drove off in Dewey's blue Buick.

He then kidnapped two men from El Centro, California, and took them with him deep into Mexico. They were still with him and unharmed over a week later when Cook was finally captured on January 15 without incident and returned to the United States. The same day, based on a tip from Cook's prison pal, Harold Martin, authorities at Joplin made a gruesome discovery. More than one thousand gawking spectators gathered on West Fourth as the bodies of the Mossers were drawn up one by one from their watery grave.

Cook at first pleaded mental blackouts and claimed to have no knowledge of having killed anyone, but he soon changed his story and confessed. While being held in California, he developed a literary bent, requesting a copy of *The Rubaiyat of Omar Khayyam,* and held forth on his uncanny marksmanship, claiming he could kill a running coyote from a moving vehicle with a single shot.

Cook was extradited to Oklahoma City, where he was convicted in the Mosser case on federal kidnapping charges and sentenced to three hundred years in Alcatraz. He was later returned to California, convicted of murdering Dewey, and sentenced to death. The "squatty killer" was executed on December 12, 1952, in the gas chamber at San Quentin. According to one reporter, he died "with a false show of boredom." His body was brought back to Joplin and buried in an unmarked grave at the Peace Church Cemetery.

Bibliography

Books and Articles

Appler, A. C. *The Younger Brothers: Their Life and Character.* 1875. Reprint, New York: Frederick Fell, Inc., 1955.

Barrett, Paul W., and Mary H. Barrett. *Young Brothers Massacre.* Columbia: University of Missouri Press, 1988.

"Benders." *Harper's Weekly,* 7 June 1873.

Brant, Marley. *The Outlaw Youngers: A Confederate Brotherhood.* Lanham, MD: Madison Books, 1992.

Castleman, Harvey. *Bald Knobbers.* Girard, KS: Haldeman-Julius Publications, 1944.

Cutler, William G. *History of the State of Kansas.* Chicago: A. T. Andreas, 1883.

Dalton Defenders Museum brochure.

Fairbanks, Jonathan, and Clyde Edwin Tuck. *Past and Present of Greene County, Missouri.* 2 vols. Indianapolis: A. W. Bowen and Company, 1915.

Farmer, Frank. "Shootout! The Facts Behind the Tragic 'Young Massacre.'" *Springfield News and Leader,* 9 January 1972.

Garton, Shirley Walker, as told to Bradley Allen Garton. *The Brookline Shoot-Out: America's Bloodiest Peace Officer Massacre.* Nixa, MO: A & J Printing, 1996.

The Graham Tragedy and the Malloy-Lee Examination: The Only Authentic History of the Murder of Sarah Graham, by Her Husband, George E. Graham, Near Springfield, Missouri, on the Night of September 30, 1885. 1886. Reprint, Springfield: Greene County Archives and Records Center, 2001.

Hanes, Bailey C. *Bill Doolin, Outlaw O. T.* Norman: University of Oklahoma Press, 1968.

Hartman, Mary, and Elmo Ingenthron. *Bald Knobbers:*

Vigilantes on the Ozarks Frontier. Gretna, LA: Pelican Publishing Company, 1988.

History of Greene County, Missouri. Edited by R. I. Holcombe. 1883. Reprint, Clinton, MO: The Printery, 1969.

History of Henry and St. Clair Counties, Missouri. 1883. Reprint, Clinton, MO: Henry County Historical Society, 1968.

History of Hickory, Polk, Cedar, Dade, and Barton Counties, Missouri. Chicago: Goodspeed Publishing Company, 1889.

History of Newton and McDonald Counties, Missouri. 1888. Reprint, Pineville, MO: McDonald County Historical Society, 1972.

Hounschell, Jim. *Lawmen and Outlaws: 116 Years in Joplin's History.* Marceline, MO: Walsworth Publishing, Co., Inc., 1989.

James, John T. *The Benders in Kansas.* 1913. Reprint, Pittsburg, KS: Mostly Books, 1995.

Kalen, Kristen, and Lynn Morrow. "Nat Kinney's Sunday School Crowd." *White River Valley Historical Quarterly* 33, no. 1 (fall 1993): 5-12.

Mahnkey, Douglas. "Troubles in Taney County." *White River Valley Historical Quarterly* 9, no. 5 (fall 1986): 2-6.

Melton, Emory. *Hanged by the Neck Until Dead.* Cassville, MO: Litho Printers, 1985.

Morris, Lucille. *Baldknobbers.* Caldwell, ID: Caxton Press, 1939.

O'Connor, Richard. *Wild Bill Hickok.* Garden City, NY: Doubleday & Company, Inc., 1959.

Pickrell, Martha M. *Emma Speaks Out: Life and Writing of Emma Molloy.* Indianapolis: Guild Press of Indiana, 2001.

"'Regulators' Formed 51 Years Ago Next May," *Springfield Leader,* 18 March 1917.

Rosa, Joseph G. "George Ward Nichols and the Legend of Wild Bill Hickok." *Arizona and the West: A Quarterly Journal of History,* 1977.

———. "'Little Dave's' Last Fight: What Really Happened When Wild Bill Hickok and Davis K. Tutt Shot It Out at Springfield, Missouri." *Quarterly of the National Association* for *Outlaw and Lawman History, Inc.* 20, no. 4, (October-December 1996).

———. *They Called Him Wild Bill.* Norman: University of Oklahoma Press, 1964.

Settle, William A., Jr. *Jesse James Was His Name.* Columbia: University of Missouri Press, 1966.

Shirley, Glenn. *Last of the Real Badmen: Henry Starr.* Lincoln: University of Nebraska Press, 1965.

———. *West of Hell's Fringe: Crime, Criminals, and the Federal Peace Officer in Oklahoma Territory, 1889-1907.* Norman: University of Oklahoma Press, 1978.

Smith, Robert Barr. "Dalton Gang's Mystery at Coffeyville." *Wild West Magazine,* October 1995.

———. *Daltons! The Raid on Coffeyville, Kansas.* Norman: University of Oklahoma Press, 1996.

Starr, Henry. *Thrilling Events: Life of Henry Starr.* 1914. Reprint, College Station, TX: Creative Publishing Company, 1982.

Wood, Fern Morrow. *The Benders: Keepers of the Devil's Inn.* Chelsea, MI: BookCrafters, 1992.

Woodside, John R. *Young Brothers Massacre.* Springfield: Springfield Publishing Co., n.d. pamphlet.

Yeatman, Ted P. *Frank and Jesse James: The Story Behind the Legend.* Nashville: Cumberland House, 2000.

Zink, Wilbur A. *The Roscoe Gun Battle: The Younger Brothers vs. Pinkerton Detectives.* Appleton City, MO: Democrat Publishing Co., 1967.

Newspapers

Baxter Springs Examiner, 1871.

Baxter Springs Herald, 1868.

Carthage (MO) Banner, various dates.

Carthage Daily Patriot, 11 August 1876.

Carthage People's Press, 26 March 1874, quoting the *Henry County Democrat.*

Carthage People's Press, 13 July 1876.

Cherokee Sentinel, 1868-70.

Chicago Tribune, 19, 22, and 24 March 1874.

Coffeyville (KS) Weekly Journal, 7 and 14 October 1892.
Columbus (KS) Workingman's Journal, 1869-70.
Fort Scott (KS) Monitor, 1869.
Fort Scott Press, 1868-69.
Fort Scott Weekly Monitor, May 1873
Galena (KS) Miner, 30 March 1878 and 9 November 1879.
Girard (KS) Press, 1869-70, 1873.
Granby (MO) Miner, 13 December 1873.
Howell County (MO) Gazette, 24 and 31 December 1931.
Independence South Kansas Tribune, March-April 1873
Joplin (MO) Daily Herald, various dates.
Joplin Globe, various dates.
Joplin Morning Herald, various dates.
Joplin News Herald, various dates.
Liberty (MO) Tribune, 27 March 1874, quoting the *Clinton (Henry County) Democrat.*
Neosho (MO) Miner & Mechanic, 12 and 30 May 1894.
Neosho (MO) Times, 2 June 1870, 13 July 1871 and 17 May 1894.
Osceola (MO) Democrat, 1874, various dates.
Peirce City (MO) Weekly Empire, 1886-87.
Pineville (MO) Herald, 21 August 1897.
St. Louis Republican, various dates.
Southwest City (MO) Enterprise, 11 May 1894, quoted in *Neosho Times,* 17 May 1894.
Springfield (MO) Daily Herald, 1887-88.
Springfield Express, various dates.
Springfield News and Leader, 3 January 1932.
Springfield Press, quoted in *Howard County Advertiser,* 28 June 1866.
Springfield Southwest Union Press, 1866.
Springfield Weekly Patriot, various dates.
Weir City (KS) Daily Sun, 1897, various dates.
West Plains (MO) Journal, 24 December 1931.

Government Documents and Other Unpublished Sources
Circuit Court Records of Greene County, Missouri, 1865-66.

Clippings about Cora Hubbard, McDonald County Library, Pineville, Missouri.

Coleman, Ramona (president of the Roscoe Community Historical Society). Interview by author. Roscoe, Missouri, 25 February 2004 and 8 March 2004.

Killion-Killian Family File, Neosho/Newton County Public Library, Neosho, Missouri.

McDonald County, Missouri, court records.

Missouri State Penitentiary Register, Missouri State Archives, Jefferson City.

Schmitt, Marilyn, comp. Notebook of clippings and transcriptions of newspaper stories about the Blalock-Fry gang. Cherokee County Historical Society Museum, Columbus, Kansas.

Union Provost Marshal file on Jacob Killian. Microfilm copy, roll F1358, Missouri State Archives, Jefferson City.

United States Census Records, 1850, 1860, 1870, 1880, various counties and states.

War of the Rebellion: A Compilation of the Official Records of the Union and Confederate Armies. Vol. 48, pt. 1. 1880-1902. Reprint, H-Bar Enterprises, 1993.

Young Brothers Massacre file. Springfield-Greene County Library, Springfield, Missouri.

Zink, Wilbur A. Telephone interview with author. 7 March 2004.

Online Sources

"Bill Doolin and His Wild Bunch." *The Wild Wild West.* http://www.gunslinger.com/doolin.html (accessed 1 October 2009).

"Bill Doolin Timeline." *The Wild Wild West.* http://www.gunslinger.com/doo-time.html (accessed 1 October 2009).

Blackmar, Frank W., ed. "Kansas: A Cyclopedia of State History, Embracing Events, Institutions, Industries, Counties, Cities, Towns, Prominent Persons, Etc." Chicago: Standard Publishing Company, 1912—*Blue Skyways,* a service of the

Kansas State Library. http://skyways.lib.ks.us/genweb/archives/1912 (accessed 1 October 2009).

Coffeyville Historical Society. http://www.coffeyville.com/Historical%20Society.htm (accessed 1 October 2009).

"Deputies Versus the Wild Bunch." United States Marshals Service. http://www.usmarshals.gov/history/dalton/doolin-dalton.htm (accessed 1 October 2009).

"Gunfight at Ingalls." *The Wild Wild West.* http://www.gunslinger.com/ingalls.html (accessed 1 October 2009).

"Soldier vs. Settler: Railroads in Southeast Kansas," Fort Scott National Historic Site. http://www.nps.gov/archive/fosc/posofsek.htm (accessed 1 October 2009).

The Soldiers Database: War of 1812-World War I. Missouri Digital Heritage, Missouri State Archives. http://www.sos.mo.gov/archives/soldiers/ (accessed 1 October 2009).

Sturges, J. A. "Illustrated History of McDonald County, Missouri." 1897. McDonald County Library. http://www.librarymail.org/genehist/sturgesbookv2_2.pdf (accessed 1 October 2009).

Tolle, Edwin, and Kevin Hatfield. "The Great Eureka Springs Bank Robbery." Eureka Springs History. http://eurekaspringshistory.com/bank_robbery_m.htm (accessed 1 October 2009).

Index